PRAISE FO

"Žižek leaves no social or cultural phenomenon untheorized, and is master of the counterintuitive observation."
—*THE NEW YORKER*

"The giant of Ljubljana provides the best intellectual high since *Anti-Oedipus*." **—*THE VILLAGE VOICE***

"The most formidably brilliant exponent of psychoanalysis, indeed of cultural theory in general, to have emerged in many decades." **—TERRY EAGLETON**

"Unafraid of confrontation and with a near limitless grasp of pop symbolism." **—*THE TIMES* (UK)**

"Žižek is a thinker who regards nothing as outside his field: the result is deeply interesting and provocative."
—*THE GUARDIAN*

"[A] great provocateur and an immensely suggestive and even dashing writer ... Žižek writes with passion and an aphoristic energy that is spellbinding."
—*LOS ANGELES TIMES*

"A relentless iconoclast, a restless wordsmith, an inventive thinker witha hatred of received wisdom." **—*BOOKFORUM***

"The Elvis of cultural theory." **—*THE NEW YORK TIMES***

EVENT

Slavoj Žižek

EVENT

A Philosophical Journey Through a Concept

MELVILLE HOUSE
BROOKLYN • LONDON

EVENT

Original edition published by Penguin Books Ltd, London
First Melville House printing: August 2014

Melville House Publishing
145 Plymouth Street
Brooklyn, NY 11201

and

8 Blackstock Mews
Islington
London N4 2BT

mhpbooks.com facebook.com/mhpbooks @melvillehouse

ISBN: 978-1-61219-411-0

Library of Congress Control Number: 2014945036

Design by Christopher King

Printed in the United States of America
1 3 5 7 9 10 8 6 4 2

To Jela
The event of my life

TIMETABLE

EVENT

ALL ABOARD

Event in Transit

'A tsunami killed more than 200,000 people in Indonesia!' 'A paparazzo snapped Britney Spears's vagina!' 'I finally realized I have to drop everything else and help him!' 'The brutal military takeover shattered the entire country!' 'The people have won! The dictator has run away!' 'How is something as beautiful as Beethoven's last piano sonata even possible?'

All these statements refer to that which at least some of us would consider an event – an amphibious notion with even more than fifty shades of grey. An 'Event' can refer to a devastating natural disaster or to the latest celebrity scandal, the triumph of the people or a brutal political change, an intense experience of a work of art or an intimate decision. Given all these variations, there is no other way to introduce order into the conundrum of definition than to take a risk, board the train and start our journey with an approximate definition of event.

Agatha Christie's *4.50 from Paddington* opens in the middle of a journey on a train from Scotland to London, where Elspeth McGillicuddy, on the way to visit her old friend Jane Marple, sees a woman being strangled in the compartment of a passing train (the 4.50 from Paddington). It all happens very fast and her vision is blurred, so the police don't take Elspeth's report seriously as there is no evidence of wrongdoing; only Miss Marple believes her story and starts to investigate. This is an event at its purest and most minimal: something shocking, out of joint that appears to happen all of a sudden and interrupts the usual flow of things; something that emerges seemingly out of nowhere, without discernible causes, an appearance without solid being as its foundation.

There is, by definition, something 'miraculous' in an event, from the miracles of our daily lives to those of the most sublime spheres, including that of the divine. The evental nature of Christianity arises from the fact that to be a Christian requires a belief in a singular event – the death and resurrection of Christ. Perhaps even more fundamental is the circular relationship between belief and its reasons: I cannot say that I believe in Christ because I was convinced by the reasons for belief; it is only when I believe that I can understand the reasons for belief. The same circular relation holds for love: I do not fall in love for precise reasons (her lips, her smile ...) – it is because I already love her that her lips, etc. attract me. This is why love, too, is evental. It is a manifestation of a circular structure in which the evental effect retroactively determines its causes or reasons.[1] And the same holds for a political event like the prolonged protests on Tahrir Square in Cairo which toppled the Mubarak regime: one can easily explain the protests as the result of specific deadlocks in Egyptian society (unemployed educated youth with no clear prospects, etc.), but somehow, none of them can really account for the synergetic energy that gave birth to what went on.

In the same way, the rise of a new art form is an event. Let us take the example of *film noir*. In his detailed analysis, Marc Vernet[2] demonstrates that all the main features that constitute the common definition of *film noir* (*chiaroscuro* lighting, askew camera angles, the paranoiac universe of the hard-boiled novel with corruption elevated to a cosmic metaphysical feature embodied in the *femme fatale*) were already present in Hollywood films. However, the enigma that remains is the mysterious efficiency and persistence of the notion of *noir*: the more Vernet is right at the level of facts, the more he offers historical causes, the more enigmatic and inexplicable becomes the extraordinary strength and longevity of this 'illusory' notion of *noir* – the notion that has haunted our imagination for decades.

At first approach, an event is thus *the effect that seems to exceed its causes* – and the *space* of an event is that which opens up by the gap that separates an effect from its causes. Already with this approximate definition, we find ourselves at the very heart of philosophy, since causality is one of the basic problems philosophy deals with: are all things connected with causal links? Does everything that exists have to be grounded in sufficient reasons? Or are there things that somehow happen out of nowhere? How, then, can philosophy help us to determine what an event – an occurrence not grounded in sufficient reasons – is and how it is possible?

From its very inception, philosophy seems to oscillate between two approaches: the transcendental and the ontological or ontic. The first concerns the universal structure of how reality appears to us. Which conditions must be met for us to perceive something as really existing? 'Transcendental' is the philosopher's technical term for such a frame, which defines the co-ordinates of reality – for example, the transcendental approach makes us aware that, for a scientific naturalist, only spatio-temporal material phenomena regulated by natural laws really exist, while for a premodern traditionalist, spirits and meanings are also part of reality, not only our human projections. The ontic approach, on the other hand, is concerned with reality itself, in its emergence and deployment: how did the universe come to be? Does it have a beginning and an end? What is our place in it? In the twentieth century, the gap between these two methods of thinking became most extreme: the transcendental approach reached its apogee with German philosopher Martin Heidegger (1889–1976), while the ontological one seems today kidnapped by natural sciences: we expect the answer to the question of the origins of our universe to come from quantum cosmology, the brain sciences and evolutionism. At the very beginning of his new bestseller, *The Grand Design*, Stephen Hawking triumphantly proclaims that 'philosophy is dead'[3]: metaphysical questions about the origin of the universe, etc., which were once the topic of philosophical speculations, can now be answered through experimental science and thus empirically tested.

What cannot but strike the traveller is that both approaches culminate in some notion of Event: the Event of the disclosure of Being – of the horizon of meaning which determines how we perceive and relate to reality – in Heidegger's thought; and in the Big Bang (or, broken symmetry), the primordial Event out of which our entire universe emerged, in the ontic approach, upheld by quantum cosmology.

Our first tentative definition of event as an effect which exceeds its causes thus brings us back to an inconsistent multiplicity: is an event a change in the way reality appears to us, or is it a shattering transformation of reality itself? Does philosophy reduce the autonomy of an event or can it account for this very autonomy? So again: is there a way to introduce some order into this conundrum? The obvious procedure would have been to classify events into species and sub-species – to distinguish between material and immaterial events, between artistic, scientific, political and intimate events, etc. However, such an approach ignores the basic feature of an event: the surprising emergence of something new which undermines every stable scheme. The only appropriate solution is thus to approach events in an evental way – to pass from one to another notion of event by way of bringing out the pervading deadlocks of each, so that our journey is one through the transformations of universality itself, coming close – so I hope – to what Hegel called 'concrete universality,' a universality 'which is not just the empty container of its particular content, but which engenders this content through the deployment of its immanent antagonisms, deadlocks and inconsistencies'.

Let us then imagine that we are on a subway trip with many stops and connections, with each stop standing for a putative definition of event. The first stop will be a change or disintegration of the frame through which reality appears to us; the second, a religious Fall. This is followed by the breaking of symmetry; Buddhist Enlightenment; an encounter with Truth that shatters our ordinary life; the experience of the self as a purely evental occurrence; the existence of illusion to truth which makes truth itself evental; a trauma which destabilizes the symbolic order we dwell in; the rise of a new

'Master-Signifier,' a signifier which structures an entire field of meaning; the experience of the pure flow of (non)sense; a radical political rupture; and the undoing of an evental achievement. The journey will be bumpy but exciting, and much will be explained along the way. So, without further ado, let's begin!

STOP 1

Framing, Reframing, Enframing

On 7 September 1944, after the Allied invasion of France, Marshal Philippe Pétain and members of his Vichy government were relocated by the Germans to Sigmaringen, a large castle in the south of Germany. An ex-territorial city-state was established there, ruled by the French government in exile nominally headed by Fernand de Brinon. There were even three embassies in the city-state: those of Germany, Italy and Japan. Sigmaringen had its own radio stations (*Radio-patrie*, *Ici la France*) and press (*La France*, *Le Petit Parisien*). The population of the Sigmaringen enclave was about 6,000 citizens, among whom were well-known collaborationist politicians (such as Laval), journalists, writers (Céline, Rebatet), actors such as Robert Le Vigan, who played Christ in Duvivier's *Golgotha* in 1935, and their families, plus around 500 soldiers, 700 French SS members and some French civilian forced labourers. The scene was one of bureaucratic madness at its extreme: in order to sustain the myth that the Vichy government was the only legitimate government of France (which, from a legal standpoint, it actually was), the state machinery continued to run at Sigmaringen, churning out an endless flow of proclamations, legal acts, administrative decisions, etc., with no actual consequences, like a state apparatus without a state, running on its own, caught up in its own fiction.[4]

Philosophy often appears to its common-sense opponents as a kind of Sigmaringen of ideas, churning out its irrelevant fictions and pretending that it offers the public insights on which the fate of humanity depends, while real life goes on somewhere else, indifferent to philosophical gigantomachias. Is philosophy really a mere theatre of shadows? A pseudo-event impotently mimicking real events? What if its power resides in its very withdrawal from direct engagement? What if, in its Sigmaringen-distance from the immediate reality of events, it can see a much more profound dimension of these same events, so that the only way to orient ourselves in the multiplicity of events is through the lens of philosophy? To answer this we must first ask: what is philosophy at its most elementary?

In February 2002, Donald Rumsfeld – at that time the U.S. Secretary of Defense – engaged in a little bit of amateur philosophizing about the relationship between the known and the unknown: 'There are known knowns; there are things we know that we know. There are known unknowns; that is to say, there are things that we now know we don't know. But there are also unknown unknowns – there are things we do not know we don't know.' The point of this exercise was to justify the impending U.S. attack on Iraq: we know what we know (say, that Saddam Hussein is the president of Iraq); we know what we don't know (how many weapons of mass destruction Saddam possesses); but there are also things we don't know that we don't know – what if Saddam possesses some other secret weapons about which we have no idea … But what Rumsfeld forgot to add was the crucial fourth term: the 'unknown knowns,' the things we don't know that we know – which is precisely the Freudian unconscious, the 'knowledge which doesn't know itself,' as the French psychoanalyst Jacques Lacan (1901–81,whose work is a basic reference of the present book[5]) used to say. (For Lacan, the Unconscious is not a pre-logical (irrational) space of instinct, but a symbolically articulated knowledge ignored by the subject.) If Rumsfeld thought that the main dangers in the confrontation with Iraq were the 'unknown unknowns,' the threats from Saddam which we cannot even suspect, our reply should have been that the main dangers were, on the contrary, the 'unknown knowns,' the disavowed beliefs and suppositions we are not even aware of adhering to ourselves. These 'unknown knowns' were indeed the main cause of the troubles the United States encountered in Iraq, and Rumsfeld's omission proves that he was not a true philosopher. 'Unknown knowns' are the privileged topic of philosophy – they form the transcendental horizon, or frame, of our experience of reality. Recall the classic topic from early modernity regarding the change of frame in our understanding of motion:

> Mediaeval physics believed that motion was caused by an impetus. Things are naturally at rest. An impetus makes something move; but then it runs out, leaving the object to slow down and stop. Something that continues moving therefore has to keep being pushed, and pushing is something you can feel. [This was even an

> argument for the existence of God, since something very big – like God – had to be pushing to keep the heavens going.] So if the Earth is moving, why don't we feel it? Copernicus could not answer that question ... Galileo had an answer for Copernicus: simple velocity is *not* felt, only acceleration is. So the earth can be moving without our feeling it. Also, velocity does not change until a force changes it. That is the idea of *inertia*, which then replaced the old idea of an impetus.[6]

This shift in our understanding of motion, from impetus to inertia, changes the very basic mode of how we relate to reality. As such, it is an event: at its most elementary, event is not something that occurs within the world, but is *a change of the very frame through which we perceive the world and engage in it*. Such a frame can sometimes be directly presented as a fiction which nonetheless enables us to tell the truth in an indirect way. A nice case of a 'truth which has the structure of a fiction' are those novels (or films) in which a play performed by characters (as part of the plot) mirrors the characters' real life amorous entanglements, such as the film about the staging of *Othello* in which the actor who plays Othello is actually jealous and, when the play's final scene is performed, really strangles the actress who plays Desdemona to death. Jane Austen's *Mansfield Park* provides an early example of this procedure. Fanny Price, a young girl from a poor family, is raised at Mansfield Park by Sir Thomas Bertram. She grows up there with her four cousins, Tom, Edmund, Maria and Julia, but is treated as inferior to them; only Edmund shows her real kindness, and, over time, a tender love grows between the two. When the children have grown up, the stern patriarch Sir Thomas leaves for a year; during this time, the fashionable and worldly Henry Crawford and his sister, Mary, arrive in the village, and their arrival sparks a series of romantic entanglements. The young people decide to put on a play, *Lovers' Vows*; Edmund and Fanny both initially oppose the plan, believing Sir Thomas would disapprove. Edmund is eventually swayed, reluctantly agreeing to play the part of Anhalt, the lover of the character played by Mary Crawford, to prevent the others bringing an outsider in to take the role. As well as giving Mary and Edmund a vehicle to talk about love and marriage, the play provides a pretext for Henry and Maria to flirt in public. To everyone's disappointment, Sir Thomas arrives unexpectedly in the middle of a rehearsal, which ends the plan.[7] But until this point, what we are witnessing is a supposed fiction standing in for a reality that nobody is willing to acknowledge.

Often, in a narrative, it is only through a similar shift of perspective that we get what the story is really is about. Much more than the famous later *WR: Mysteries of the Organism*, Dušan Makavejev's masterpiece is *Innocence Without Protection* (1968), with its unique structure of a 'film within a film'. Its hero is Dragoljub Aleksić, an ageing Serbian air acrobat who performed his acrobatics hanging from aeroplanes, and who, during the wartime German occupation of Serbia, shot a ridiculously sentimental melodrama in Belgrade with the same title. Makavejev's film includes this film in its entirety, adding interviews with Aleksić and other documentary shots, and the key to the film is the relationship between these two levels and the question they pose: whose innocence is without protection? Aleksić's film answers: the girl whom Aleksić saves from the machinations of her evil stepmother and the man she wants to impose on her as husband. However, the true answer is: the 'innocence unprotected' is that of Aleksić himself, persisting in his dangerous acrobatics until his late age, posing with his body for the camera, acting and singing, victimized and made fun of by Germans, then by post-war Communists, and finally by the film's spectators themselves, who cannot but laugh at his ridiculously naïve performances. The more Makavejev's film progresses, the more we become aware of the pathos of Aleksić's unconditional fidelity to his acrobatic mission. What can be more ridiculously tragic than to see an old man in his basement, hanging by his teeth on a chain and swinging his torso for the camera? Does he not expose himself in this way to the public gaze in all his innocence, without the means to protect himself from the ridicule of the public? This shift in our perspective, when we become aware that the true innocence to be protected is Aleksić's, despite him supposedly being our hero, designates the evental moment of the film. It is the exposure of the reality that nobody wanted to admit, but which has now become a revelation, and has changed the playing field.

In Hollywood, the mother of all frames is, of course, the coming together of a couple. Here is how the Wikipedia entry describes the final scene of the Spielberg sci-fi thriller *Super 8*: 'The movie ends with the star ship blasting off towards the creature's home planet while Joe and Alice hold hands.' The couple comes together – is 'created' – when the Thing, which Lacan would refer to as 'the traumatic third,' and which served as the ambiguous obstacle to the couple's creation, is finally defeated and disappears. The role of the obstacle is ambiguous because although it may be sinister, it is nonetheless needed to bring the couple together in the first place; it is the challenge they must face or the obstacle they must overcome in order to realize they want to be together.[8]

How can we undermine this narrative frame which subordinates the encounter with a Thing to the production of a couple? Let us take Stanislaw Lem's classic science fiction novel *Solaris* and its 1972 cinema version by Andrei Tarkovsky. *Solaris* is the story of a space agency psychologist, Kelvin, sent to a half-abandoned spaceship above a newly discovered planet, Solaris, where, recently, strange things have been taking place (scientists go mad, hallucinate, kill themselves). Solaris is a planet with an oceanic fluid surface which moves incessantly and, from time to time, imitates recognizable forms, not only elaborate geometric structures, but also gigantic child bodies or real-life buildings. Although all attempts to communicate with the planet fail, scientists entertain the hypothesis that Solaris is a gigantic brain which somehow reads our minds. Soon after his arrival, Kelvin finds at his side in his bed his dead wife, Harey, who, years ago on Earth, killed herself after he had abandoned her. He is unable to shake Harey off, all attempts to get rid of her fail miserably (after he sends her into space with a rocket, she rematerializes the next day); and analysis of her tissue demonstrates that she is not composed of atoms like normal human beings. Beneath a certain micro-level, there is nothing, just void. Finally, Kelvin grasps that Solaris, this gigantic Brain, directly materializes our innermost fantasies which support our desire; it is a machine that materializes in reality my ultimate fantasmatic object that I would never be ready to accept in reality, though my entire psychic life turns around it. Harey is a materialization of Kelvin's innermost traumatic fantasies.

Read in this way, the story is really about the hero's inner journey, about his attempt to come to terms with his repressed truth, or, as Tarkovsky himself said: 'Maybe, effectively, the mission of Kelvin on Solaris has only one goal: to show that love of the other is indispensable to all life. A man without love is no longer a man. The aim of the entire "solaristic" is to show humanity must be love.' In clear contrast to this, Lem's novel focuses on the inert external presence of the planet Solaris, of this 'Thing which thinks' (to use Kant's expression, which fully fits here): the point of the novel is precisely that Solaris remains an impenetrable Other, with no possible communication with us. True, it returns to us our innermost disavowed fantasies, but the 'What do you want?' beneath this act remains thoroughly impenetrable (Why does It do it? As a purely mechanical response? To play demonic games with us? To help us – or compel us – to confront our dis-avowed truth?). It would be interesting to compare Tarkovsky's work with the Hollywood commercial rewritings of novels which have served as bases for movies: Tarkovsky does exactly the same as the lowest Hollywood producer, reinscribing the enigmatic encounter with Otherness, the Thing, into the framework of the production of the couple.

The way to break out of the Hollywood frame is thus not to treat the Thing as just a metaphor of family tension, but to accept it in its meaningless and impenetrable presence. This is what happens in Lars von Trier's *Melancholia* (2011), which stages an interesting reversal of this classic formula of an object-Thing (an asteroid, alien) which serves as the enabling obstacle to the creation of the couple: at the film's end, the Thing (a planet on a collision course with Earth) does not withdraw, as in *Super 8*; it hits the Earth, destroying all life, and the film is about the different ways the main characters deal with the impending catastrophe (with responses ranging from suicide to cynical acceptance). The planet is thus the Thing – *das Ding* at its purest, as Heidegger would have it: the Real Thing which dissolves any symbolic frame – we see it, it is our death, we cannot do anything.[9] The film begins with an introductory sequence, shot in slow motion, involving the main characters and images from space that introduces the visual motifs. A shot from the vantage point of space shows a giant planet approaching Earth; the two planets collide. The film continues in two parts, each named for one of two sisters, Justine and Claire.

In part one, 'Justine,' a young couple, Justine and Michael, are at their wedding reception at the mansion of Justine's sister, Claire, and her husband John. The lavish reception lasts from dusk to dawn with eating, drinking, dancing and the usual family conflicts (Justine's bitter mother makes sarcastic and insulting remarks, ultimately resulting in John attempting to throw her off his property; Justine's boss follows her around, begging her to write a piece of advertising copy for him). Justine drifts away from the party and becomes increasingly distant; she has sex with a stranger on the lawn, and at the end of the party, Michael leaves her.

In part two, 'Claire,' the ill, depressed Justine comes to stay with Claire and John and their son, Leo. Although Justine is unable to carry out normal everyday activities like taking a bath or even eating, she gets better over time. During her stay, Melancholia, a massive blue telluric planet that had before been hidden behind the sun, becomes visible in the sky as it approaches Earth. John, who is an amateur astronomer, is excited about the planet, and looks forward to the 'fly-by' expected by scientists, who have assured the public that Earth and Melancholia will pass each other without colliding. But Claire is getting fearful and believes the end of the world is imminent. On the internet, she finds a site describing the movements of Melancholia around Earth as a 'dance of death,' in which the apparent passage of Melancholia past Earth initiates a slingshot orbit that will bring the planets into collision soon after. On the night of the fly-by, it seems that Melancholia will not hit Earth; however, after the fly-by, background birdsong abruptly ceases, and the next day, Claire realizes that Melancholia is circling back and will collide with Earth after all. John, who also discovers that the end is near, commits suicide through a pill overdose. Claire becomes increasingly agitated, while Justine remains unperturbed by the impending doom: calm and silent, she accepts the coming event, claiming that she knows that life does not exist elsewhere in the universe. She comforts Leo by making a protective 'magic cave,' a symbolic shelter of wooden sticks, on the mansion's lawn. Justine, Claire and Leo enter the shelter as the planet approaches. Claire continues to remain agitated and fearful, while Justine and Leo stay calm and hold hands. The three are instantly incinerated as the collision occurs and destroys Earth.

This narrative is interspersed with numerous ingenious details. To calm Claire, John tells her to look at Melancholia through a circle of wire which just encompasses its circular shape in the sky, thus enframing it, and to repeat this 10 minutes later so she will see that the shape has become smaller, leaving gaps within the frame – a proof that Melancholia is moving away from the Earth. She does this, and grows jubilant when she sees a smaller shape. However, when she looks at Melancholia through the frame some hours later, she is terrified to see that the shape of the planet has now expanded well beyond the frame of the wire circle. This circle is the circle of fantasy enframing reality, and the shock arrives when the Thing breaks through and spills over into reality. There are also wonderful details of the disturbances that happen in nature as Melancholia approaches the Earth: insects, worms, roaches and all other repellent forms of life usually hidden beneath the green grass come to the surface, rendering visible the disgusting crawling of life beneath the idyllic surface – the Real invading reality, ruining its image. (Similarly David Lynch's *Blue Velvet*, in which, in a famous shot after the father's heart attack, the camera moves extremely close to the grass surface and then penetrates it, rendering visible the crawling of micro-life, the repelling real beneath the idyllic suburban surface.)[10]

The idea for *Melancholia* originated in a therapy session von Trier attended during treatment for depression: the psychiatrist told him that depressive people tend to act more calmly than others under extreme pressure or the threat of catastrophe – they already expect bad things to happen. This fact offers yet another example of the split between reality – the social universe of established customs and opinions in which we dwell – and the traumatic meaningless brutality of the Real: in the film, John is a 'realist,' fully immersed in ordinary reality, so when the co-ordinates of this reality dissolve, his entire world breaks down; Claire is an hysteric who starts to question everything in a panic, but nonetheless avoids complete psychotic breakdown; and the depressed Justine goes on as usual because she is already living in a melancholic withdrawal from reality.

The film deploys four subjective attitudes towards this ultimate Event (the planet-Thing hitting the Earth) as Lacan would understand them. John, the husband, is the embodiment of *university knowledge*, which falls apart in its encounter with the Real; Leo, the son, is clearly the object of concern, or *desire*, for the other three; Claire is the *hysterical* woman, the only full subject in the film (insofar as subjectivity means doubts, questioning, inconsistency); and this, surprisingly, leaves to Justine the position of a *Master*, the one who stabilizes a situation of panic and chaos by presenting a new Master-Signifier, which introduces order into a confused situation, conferring on it the stability of meaning. Her Master-Signifier is the 'magic cave' that she builds to establish a protected space when the Thing approaches. One should be very careful here: Justine is not a protective Master who offers a beautiful lie – in other words, she is not the Roberto Benigni character in *Life Is Beautiful*.[11] What she provides is a symbolic fiction which, of course, has no magic efficacy, but which works at its proper level of preventing panic. Justine's point is not to blind us from the impending catastrophe: the 'magic cave' enables us to joyously accept the End. There is nothing morbid in it; such an acceptance is, on the contrary, the necessary background of concrete social engagement.[12] Justine is thus the only one who is able to propose an appropriate answer to the impending catastrophe, and to the total obliteration of every symbolic frame.

To grasp properly the acceptance of such radical End, one

should risk a comparison between Trier's *Melancholia* and Terrence Malick's *The Tree of Life* (released in the same year). The story of both films involves the same two levels: family trauma versus cosmic catastrophe. Although one cannot be but repelled by *The Tree of Life*'s excessive pseudo-spirituality, the film contains some interesting moments.[13] It opens with a line from the Book of Job, God's answer to Job's complaint about why all the misfortunes have hit him: 'Where were you when I laid the foundations of the earth ... while the morning stars sang together?' (38:4, 7) These lines obviously refer to the O'Brien family, which finds itself in a Job-like position of suffering an undeserved catastrophe: at the beginning of *The Tree of Life*, Mrs O'Brien receives a telegram informing her of the death of her son, RL, aged nineteen; Mr O'Brien is also notified, by telephone while at an airport, and the family is thrown into turmoil. How are we to read this series of rhetorical questions offered by God as the reply to Job's question of why the misfortunes hit him? Similarly, how are we to understand the tragedy that befalls the O'Briens? In his review of the film, David Wolpe points out the ambiguity of God's reply:

> God's recounting of the wonders of nature can be seen in one of two ways. One possibility is that the immensity of the natural world, in its merciless indifference, has nothing to do with the concerns of human beings. The desert does not care if you pray, and the rushing cataract will not pause for pity. Nature shows its blank, grand face to us, and we are nothing. Indeed Job recants of his protest, proclaiming 'for I am but dust and ashes.' ... But gradually we see that each image, from

> the cell to the cosmos, is not only grand, it is beautiful. The second half of the quote from Job, how the morning stars sing, reminds us that the appreciation of wonder and beauty is also possible. We may lose our ego in nature's indifference, but we may also lose it in nature's magnificence. Do we see the world as heartless or as sublime? The drama of our life and death is fleeting, but it is played out on a stage of unparalleled wonder.[14]

The most radical reading of Job was proposed in the 1930s by the Norwegian theologian Peter Wessel Zapffe, who accentuated Job's 'boundless perplexity' when God himself finally appears to him: expecting a sacred and pure God whose intellect is infinitely superior to ours, Job 'finds himself confronted with a world ruler of grotesque primitiveness, a cosmic cave-dweller, a braggart and blusterer, almost agreeable in his total ignorance of spiritual culture … What is new for Job is *not* God's greatness in quantifiable terms; that he knew fully in advance … ; what is new is the qualitative baseness.'[15] In other words, God – the God of the Real – is *das Ding*, a capricious cruel master who simply has no sense of universal justice. So where does *The Tree of Life* stand with regard to these readings?

Malick relies on the link between trauma and fantasy: one of the possible reactions to a trauma is the escape into fantasy, i.e., to imagine the world in itself, outside our subjective horizon. He shows us the universe being formed, including the Milky Way and the Solar System. Voices ask various existential questions. On the newly formed Earth, volcanoes erupt and microbes begin to form. Early sea life is shown, then plants on the land, then dinosaurs. From the vantage point of space, an asteroid is seen hitting the Earth ... This logic recently reached its climax in Alan Weisman's book *The World Without Us*, a vision of what would have happened if humanity (and *only* humanity) were suddenly to disappear from the earth – natural diversity blooming again, nature gradually overgrowing human artefacts. In imagining the world without us, we, humans, are reduced to a pure disembodied gaze observing our own absence, and, as Lacan pointed out, this is the fundamental subjective position of fantasy: to observe the world in the condition of the subject's non-existence (the fantasy of witnessing the act of one's own conception, the parental copulation, or of witnessing one's own burial, like Tom Sawyer and Huck Finn). *The World Without Us* is thus fantasy at its purest: witnessing the Earth itself retaining its pre-castrated state of innocence, before we humans spoiled it with our hubris.

So while *The Tree of Life* escapes into a similar cosmic fantasy of a world without us, *Melancholia* does not do the same. It does not imagine the end of the world in order to escape from family deadlock: Justine really is melancholic, deprived of the fantasmatic gaze. That is to say, melancholy is, at its most radical, not the failure of the work of mourning, the persisting attachment to the lost object, but their very opposite: 'melancholy offers the paradox of an intention to mourn that precedes and anticipates the loss of the object'.[16] Therein resides the melancholic's stratagem: the only way to possess an object that we never had, which was from the very outset lost, is to treat an object that we still fully possess as if this object is already lost. This is what provides a unique flavour to a melancholic love relationship, such as the one between Newland and Countess Olenska in Wharton's *The Age of Innocence*: although the partners are still together, immensely in love, enjoying each other's presence, the shadow of the future separation already colours their relationship, so that they perceive their current pleasures under the aegis of the catastrophe (separation) to come. In this precise sense, melancholy effectively is the beginning of philosophy – and in this precise sense, Justine from *Melancholia* is *not* melancholic: her loss is the absolute loss, the end of the world, and what Justine mourns in advance is this absolute loss – she is literally living in the end time. When catastrophe was just a threat of catastrophe, she was merely a depressed melancholic; once the threat is here, she finds herself in her element.

And here we reach the limit of *event as reframing*: in *Melancholia*, the event is no longer a mere *change* of frame, *it is the destruction of frame as such*, i.e., the disappearance of humanity, the material support of every frame. But is such a total destruction the only way to acquire a distance from the frame that regulates our access to reality? The psychoanalytic name for this frame is fantasy, so the question can also be put in the terms of fantasy: can we acquire a distance towards our fundamental fantasy, or, as Lacan put it, can we traverse our fantasy?

The concept of fantasy needs to be further elaborated here. Common wisdom tells us that, according to psychoanalysis, whatever we are doing, we are secretly thinking about THAT. Sex is the universal hidden reference behind every activity. However, the true Freudian question is: what are we thinking when we *are* doing THAT? It is the real sex itself which, in order to be palatable, has to be sustained by some fantasy. The logic is here the same as that of a Native American tribe whose members have discovered that all dreams have some hidden sexual meaning – all, *except the overtly sexual ones*: here, precisely, one has to look for another meaning. Any contact with a 'real,' flesh-and-blood other, any sexual pleasure that we find in touching *another* human being, is not something evident, but something inherently traumatic – shattering, intrusive, potentially disgusting – for the subject, something that can be sustained only insofar as this other enters the subject's fantasy frame.

So, what is fantasy? Fantasy does not simply realize a desire in a hallucinatory way; rather it constitutes our desire, provides its co-ordinates – it literally *teaches us how to desire*. To put it in somewhat simplified terms: fantasy does not mean that, when I desire a strawberry cake and cannot get it in reality, I fantasize about eating it; the problem is rather, *how do I know that I desire a strawberry cake in the first place? This* is what fantasy tells me. This role of fantasy hinges on the fact that, as Lacan would have it, there is no universal formula or matrix guaranteeing a harmonious sexual relationship with one's partner: every subject has to invent a fantasy of his own, a 'private' formula for the sexual relationship.

The topic of a fantasy that sustains a sexual relationship takes a weird turn in Ernst Lubitsch's *Broken Lullaby* (1932). The film's original title, *The Man I Killed*, was first changed to *The Fifth Commandment* to avoid giving the 'wrong impressions in the minds of the public about the character of the story'. Haunted by the memory of Walter Holderlin, a soldier he killed during the Great War, a French musician, Paul Renard, travels to Germany to find his family, using the address on a letter he found on the dead man's body. Because anti-French sentiment continues to permeate Germany, Dr Holderlin initially refuses to welcome Paul into his home, but changes his mind when his dead son's fiancée, Elsa, identifies him as the man who has been leaving flowers on Walter's grave. Rather than reveal the real connection between them, Paul tells the Holderlin family he was a friend of their son's who attended the same musical conservatory that he did. Although the hostile townspeople and local gossips disapprove, the Holderlins befriend Paul, who falls in love with Elsa. When she shows Paul her former fiancé's bedroom, he becomes distraught and tells her the truth. She convinces him not to confess to Walter's parents, who have embraced him as their second son, and Paul agrees to forego easing his conscience and stays with his adopted family. Dr Holderlin presents Walter's violin to Paul. In the film's final scene, Paul plays the violin while Elsa accompanies him on the piano, both of them observed by the parental couple with loving gazes ... No wonder film critic Pauline Kael dismissed the film, claiming that Lubitsch 'mistook drab, sentimental hokum for ironic, poetic tragedy'.[17] There is effectively something disturbing here, a weird oscillation between poetic melodrama and obscene humour. The couple (the girl and the killer of her previous fiancé) are happily united under the protective gaze of the dead fiancé's parents – and it is this gaze that provides the fantasy frame for their relationship.

Insofar as fantasy provides the frame which enables us to experience the real of our lives as a meaningful Whole, the disintegration of a fantasy can have disastrous consequences. A loss of the fantasmatic frame is often experienced in the midst of intense sexual activity – one is passionately engaged in the act when, all of a sudden, one as it were loses contact, disengages, begins to observe oneself from outside and becomes aware of the mechanistic nonsense of one's repetitive movements. In such moments, the fantasmatic frame which sustained the intensity of enjoyment disintegrates, and we are confronted with the ludicrous real of copulation.[18]

What psychoanalysis aims at is not such a disintegration of fantasy, but something different and much more radical, the *traversing* of fantasy. And while it may seem obvious that psychoanalysis should liberate us from the hold of idiosyncratic fantasies and enable us to confront reality the way it is, this is precisely what Lacan does *not* have in mind: traversing the fantasy does not mean simply going outside fantasy, but shattering its foundations, accepting its inconsistency. In our daily existence, we are immersed in 'reality,' structured and supported by the fantasy, but this very immersion makes us blind to the fantasy frame which sustains our access to reality. To 'traverse the fantasy' therefore means, paradoxically, *to fully identify oneself with the fantasy*, to bring the fantasy out – in Richard Boothby's succinct formulation:

> 'Traversing the fantasy' thus does not mean that the subject somehow abandons its involvement with fanciful caprices and accommodates itself to a pragmatic 'reality,' but precisely the opposite: the subject is submitted to that effect of the symbolic lack that reveals the limit of everyday reality. To traverse the fantasy in

> the Lacanian sense is to be more profoundly claimed by the fantasy than ever, in the sense of being brought into an ever more intimate relation with that real core of the fantasy that transcends imaging.[19]

How are we to read this paradox of traversing the fantasy by way of over-identifying with it? Let us make a detour through two exemplary movies: Neil Jordan's *The Crying Game* (1992), and David Cronenberg's *M. Butterfly* (1993). In spite of their fundamentally different characters, both films tell the story of a man passionately in love with a beautiful woman who turns out to be a man dressed up as a woman (the transvestite in *The Crying Game*, the opera singer in *M. Butterfly*), and the central scene of both films is the traumatic confrontation of the man with the fact that the object of his love is also a man. Here, of course, the obvious objection awaits us: does *M. Butterfly* not offer a tragicomic confused bundle of male fantasies about women, not a true relationship with a woman? The entire action of the film takes place among men. Does not the grotesque incredibility of the plot simultaneously mask and point towards the fact that what we are dealing with is a case of homosexual love for the transvestite? The film is simply dishonest, and refuses to acknowledge this obvious fact. This elucidation, however, fails to address the true enigma of *M. Butterfly* (and of *The Crying Game*): how can a hopeless love between the hero and his partner, a man dressed up as a woman, realize the notion of heterosexual love far more authentically than a 'normal' relationship with a woman? Or, with regard to *The Crying Game*: why is the confrontation with the lover's body such a trauma? Not because the subject encounters something alien, but because he confronts there the core fantasy that sustains his desire. The 'heterosexual' love for a woman is actually homosexual, sustained by the fantasy that the woman is a man dressed up as a woman. Here we can see what traversing the fantasy can mean: not to see through it and perceive the reality obfuscated by it, but to directly confront the fantasy as such. Once we do this, its hold over us is suspended – why? Because fantasy remains operative only insofar as it functions as the transparent background of our experience – fantasy is like a dirty intimate secret which cannot survive public exposure.

This bring us to Heidegger: when Heidegger speaks about the 'essence of technology,' he has in mind something like the frame of a fundamental fantasy which, as a transparent background, structures the way we relate to reality. *Gestell*, Heidegger's word for the essence of technology, is usually translated into English as 'enframing'. At its most radical, technology does not designate a complex network of machines and activities, but the *attitude towards reality* which we assume when we are engaged in such activities: technology is the way reality discloses itself to us in contemporary times. The paradox of technology as the concluding moment of Western metaphysics is that it is a mode of enframing which poses a danger to enframing itself: the human being reduced to an object of technological manipulation is no longer properly human; it loses the very feature of being ecstatically open to reality. However, this danger also contains the potential for salvation: the moment we become aware and fully assume the fact that technology itself is, in its essence, a mode of enframing, we overcome it – this is Heidegger's version of traversing the fantasy.

And this then brings us to Heidegger's notion of Event (*Ereignis*): for Heidegger, Event has nothing to do with processes that go on out there in reality. Event designates a new epochal disclosure of Being, the emergence of a new 'world' (a horizon of meaning within which all entities appear). Catastrophe thus occurs before the (f)act: catastrophe is not the atomic self-destruction of humanity, but the relation to nature which reduces it to its techno-scientific exploitation. Catastrophe is not our ecological ruin, but the loss of home-roots which renders possible the ruthless exploitation of the earth. Catastrophe is not that we are reduced to automata manipulated by biogenetics, but the very approach which renders this prospect possible. Even the possibility of total self-destruction is just a consequence of our relating to nature as a collection of objects of technological exploitation. This brings us to our next stop: from Event as enframing – as a shift in our relationship to reality – to Event as a radical change of this reality itself.

STOP 2

Felix Culpa

In Plato's arguably greatest dialogue, *Parmenides*, Parmenides raises a question that perplexes Socrates and forces him to admit his limitation: are there also ideas of lowest material things, ideas of shit, of dust? Is there an *eidos* – an eternal ideal form – for 'things that might seem absurd, like hair and mud and dirt, or anything else totally undignified and worthless?' (130c) What lurks behind this question is not only the embarrassing fact that the noble notion of Form could also apply to excremental objects, but a much more precise paradox that Plato approaches in his *Statesman* (262a–263a), in which he makes a crucial claim: divisions (of a genus into species) should be made at the proper joints. For example, it is a mistake to divide the genus of all human beings into Greeks and barbarians: 'barbarian' is not a proper form because it does not designate a positively defined group (species), but merely all persons who are not Greeks. The positivity of the term 'barbarian' thus conceals the fact that it serves as the container for all those who do not fit the form 'Greek'. But what if this holds for all divisions of genera into species? What if every genus, in order to be fully divided into species, has to include such a negative pseudo-species, a 'part of no part' of the genus? All those who belong to the genus but are not covered by any of its species? If this sounds abstract, recall numerous examples from the history of science, from the imaginary combustion element phlogiston (a pseudo-concept that merely betrayed scientists' ignorance of how light effectively travels) to Marx's 'Asiatic mode of production' – another sort of negative container: the only true content of this concept would be something like 'all the modes of production which do not fit Marx's standard categorization of the modes of production'. That is to say, how did Marx arrive at this concept? First, he articulated the Eurocentrist series of progressive modes of production: pre-class tribal society, ancient slavery, feudalism, capitalism, Communism; then, after noticing that many ancient societies, from China and Egypt to the Inca empire, did not fit any of these modes, he constructed a new category – 'Asiatic modes of production' – which appears to be a consistent concept, but is actually just an empty container for all such unfitting elements.

So what has this additional concept which disturbs the clarity of rational classification of the division of a genus into its species to do with the topic of Event? Or more specifically: with the event as *culpa*, Fall? Everything. In principle, we can distinguish between a rational structure, an atemporal classification of a totality into its species and sub-species, and its imperfect temporal actualization in contingent material reality. There may be surpluses in both directions – there may be formal possibilities which are not actualized, empty slots in a structure (say, there are four types of houses logically possible, but for contingent reasons, only three of them are actually built), or there may be a wealth of empirical formations which do not fit any of the categories allowed by the classification. However, the paradoxical negative container is something quite different from both these cases: it represents within the structure of classification, as one of its elements, that which escapes this structure, i.e., it is the point of inscription of historical contingency into a formal structure, the point at which the formal structure, as it were, falls into its content, into contingent reality. And, insofar as the formal structure is in itself atemporal while the level of contingent reality is evental – i.e., the domain of contingent events, of constant change, generation and corruption – the negative container is also the point at which event intervenes (or is inscribed) into the formal structure. The place of this surplus, excessive element can be discerned through the imbalance between the universal and the particular – here is its most famous example, Kierkegaard's immortal 1843 division of mankind:

> A wit has said that one might divide mankind into officers, serving maids, and chimney sweeps. To my mind this remark is not only witty but profound, and it would require a great speculative talent to devise a better classification. When a classification does not ideally exhaust its object, a haphazard classification is altogether preferable, because it sets imagination in motion.[20]

True, the chimney-sweeper element is a particular supplement which provides the specific colouring of the preceding terms (what they 'really mean' in the concrete historical totality); however, this is not to be read as if the chimney-sweeper element stands for the touch of common sense, as in Heinrich Heine's (a contemporary of Kierkegaard's) well-known saying that one should value above everything else 'freedom, equality and crab soup'. 'Crab soup' stands here for all the small pleasures in the absence of which we become (mental, if not real) terrorists, following an abstract idea and enforcing it on to reality without any consideration of concrete circumstances. One should emphasize here that such a 'wisdom' is precisely what Kierkegaard did *not* have in mind – his message is rather the opposite one: the principle itself, in its purity, is already coloured by the particularity of crab soup, i.e., the particularity sustains the very purity of the principle.

The excessive element is thus a supplement to the Two, to the harmonious couple, *yin* and *yang*, the two classes, etc.; for example, capitalist, worker, *and the Jew*; or, maybe, high class, low class, *plus rabble*.[21] (In the triad of officer, maid and the chimney sweeper, the chimney sweeper can effectively be perceived as Freud's *Liebesstoerer*, the obscene intruder who cuts short the couple's love-making. In fact, let us go to the end and imagine the ultimate obscenity: a sexual act between the officer and the maid, with the chimney sweeper who intervenes afterwards with the act of belated contraception, cleaning up her 'channel' with his brush ...[22])

The excess of the universal over its actual particularities thus points towards a weird excessive particular element, as in G. K. Chesterton's well-known remark addressed at 'my readers most of whom are human' – or, as a well-known soccer player once put it after an important match: 'My gratitude goes to my parents, especially my mom and my dad.' Who is then the remaining parent, the third one, neither mother nor father? Walter Benjamin touched on something similar in his early esoteric essay 'On Language as Such and on the Language of Man'[23]: his point is not that language as such is to be divided into many species – language of humans, of animals, of genetics, etc. There is only one actually existing language, the language of humans, and the tension between language in its universality ('as such') and actual particularity (language effectively spoken by humans) is inscribed into the language of humans, splitting it from within. In other words, even if there is only one language, we still have to distinguish between the universal (language as such) and the particular (human language) – language is a genus with only one species, itself as a particular actual language. This brings us back to the notion of Fall: 'human language' designates the Fall of the divine 'language as such,' its contamination with all the filth of envy, power struggle, and obscenity. And it is easy to see in what sense this Fall is evental: in it, the eternal structure of divine language becomes integrated into the evental flux of human history.

This takes us on to theology, and more precisely, to the theological topic of the Fall. As it was made clear by Søren Kierkegaard (1813–55), Danish theologian and philosopher, Christianity is the first and only religion of the Event: the only access to the Absolute (God) is through our acceptance of the unique event of Incarnation as a singular historical occurrence. This is why Kierkegaard says it is Christ versus Socrates: Socrates stands for remembrance, for rediscovering the higher reality of Ideas which are always already in us, while Christ announces the 'good news' of a radical break. This is *event as rupture in the normal run of things*, as the miracle of 'Christ has risen'. However, we should not take resurrection as something that happens *after* Christ's death, but as the obverse of the death itself – Christ is alive as the Holy Ghost, as the love that binds the community of believers.[24] In short, 'Christ has risen' effectively means exactly the same as 'Christ has fallen':

in other religions, man falls from God (into sinful terrestrial life), only in Christianity does God himself fall. But how? From where? The only possibility is: from himself, into his own creation.[25]

To put it in mystical terms, the Christian Event is the exact opposite of a 'return to innocence': it is the Original Sin itself, the primordial pathological choice of the unconditional attachment to some singular object (like falling in love with a person who, thereafter, matters to us more than everything else). This choice is pathological because it is literally unbalanced: it destroys the preceding indifference; it introduces division, pain and suffering. In Buddhist terms, a Christian event is the exact structural obverse of Enlightenment, of attaining Nirvana: it is the very gesture by means of which false appearance and suffering emerge in the world. The Christian Event of 'incarnation' is thus not so much the time when ordinary temporal reality touches Eternity, but rather the time when Eternity reaches into time. Chesterton saw this very clearly and rejected the fashionable claim about the 'alleged spiritual identity of Buddhism and Christianity':

> Love desires personality; therefore love desires division. It is the instinct of Christianity to be glad that God has broken the universe into little pieces ... This is the intellectual abyss between Buddhism and Christianity; that for the Buddhist or Theosophist personality is the fall of man, for the Christian it is the purpose of God, the whole point of his cosmic idea. The world-soul of the Theosophists asks man to love it only in order that man may throw himself into it. But the divine

> centre of Christianity actually threw man out of it in order that he might love it ... all modern philosophies are chains which connect and fetter; Christianity is a sword which separates and sets free. No other philosophy makes God actually rejoice in the separation of the universe into living souls.[26]

The consequences of this priority of the Fall are unexpected and harsh – if the Fall is the condition of the Good and, as such, a 'happy fall' (*felix culpa*), then the agent of the Fall (Eve, the woman, who seduced Adam into sin) is the original ethical agent. Traces of misogyny in Christian tradition should thus not deceive us – upon a closer look, they reveal themselves to be deeply ambiguous. Here is the early Christian thinker Tertullian (*c.*160–*c.*225) at his misogynist worst, addressing women:

> Do you not know that you are *each* an Eve? The sentence of God on this sex of yours lives in this age: the guilt must of necessity live too. You are the devil's gateway: you are the unsealer of that (forbidden) tree: you are the first deserter of the divine law: you are she who persuaded him whom the devil was not valiant enough to attack. You destroyed so easily God's image, man *Adam*. Because of what you deserve – that is, death – even the Son of God had to die.[27]

But is the last line not profoundly ambiguous? This ambiguity is similar to the one we encountered in the autumn of 2006 when Sheikh Taj el-Din al-Hilali, Australia's most senior

Muslim cleric, caused a scandal after a group of Muslim men had been jailed for gang rape by saying: 'If you take uncovered meat and place it outside on the street ... and the cats come and eat it ... whose fault is it – the cats or the uncovered meat? The uncovered meat is the problem.' The explosive nature of this comparison between a woman who is not veiled and raw, uncovered meat distracted attention from another, much more surprising premise underlying Sheikh Hilali's argument: if women are held responsible for the sexual conduct of men, does this not imply that men are totally helpless when faced with what they perceive as a sexual provocation, that they are simply unable to resist, that they are totally enslaved to their sexual hunger, precisely like a cat when it sees raw meat? In other words, does it not imply that brutal rapist men act as if they are still in Paradise, beyond good and evil? Similarly, is Eve not the only true partner of God in the affair of the Fall? The act (the catastrophic decision) is hers: she opens up the path towards the recognition of the difference between good and evil (which is the consequence of the Fall) and towards the shame of being naked – in short, the path towards the human universe. All one should do here to grasp the true situation is to bear in mind Hegel's (rather obvious) point: the innocence of the 'paradise' is another name for animal life, so that what the Bible calls 'Fall' is nothing more than the passage from animal life to human existence proper. *It is thus the Fall itself which creates the dimension from which it is the Fall* – or, as St Augustine put it long ago (in his *Enchiridion*, xxvii): 'God judged it better to bring good out of evil, than to allow no evil to exist.'

One has to be careful here not to succumb to the perverse

reading of the priority of the Fall – what, exactly, does perversion mean here? A short-circuit in which I myself cause the Evil so that I can overcome it by my struggle for the Good, like the mad governess from Patricia Highsmith's short story 'Heroine,' who sets the family house on fire in order to be able to prove her devotion to the family by bravely saving the children from the raging fire. The most radical case of such a perverse reading was provided by Nicolas Malebranche (1638–1715), the great Cartesian Catholic who was excommunicated after his death and his books destroyed on account of his very excessive orthodoxy. Malebranche laid the cards on the table and 'revealed the secret' of Christianity; his Christology is based on an answer to the question, 'Why did God create the world?' – So that He could bask in the glory of being celebrated by His creation. God wanted recognition, and He knew that, for recognition, I need another subject to recognize me; so He created the world out of pure selfish vanity.

Consequently, it was not that Christ came down to Earth in order to deliver people from sin, from the legacy of Adam's Fall; on the contrary, *Adam had to fall in order to enable Christ to come down to earth and dispense salvation*. Malebranche applies here to God Himself the 'psychological' insight which tells us that the saintly figure who sacrifices himself for the benefit of others, to deliver them from their misery, secretly *wants* the others to suffer *so that he will be able to help them* – like the proverbial husband who works all day for his poor crippled wife, yet would probably abandon her if she were to regain her health and become a successful career woman. It is much more satisfying to sacrifice oneself for the poor victim than to enable the other to lose the status of a victim, and perhaps become even more successful than ourselves ... Malebranche develops this parallel to its conclusion, to the horror of the Jesuits who organized his excommunication. God also ultimately *loves only himself*, and merely uses man to promulgate His own glory. It is not true that, if Christ had not come to earth to deliver humanity, everyone would have been lost – quite the contrary; *nobody* would have been lost, i.e., *every* human being had to fall so that Christ could come and deliver *some* of them. Malebranche's conclusion here is shattering: since the death of Christ is a key step in realizing the goal of creation, at no time was God (the Father) happier than when he was observing His son suffering and dying on the Cross.

The only way to truly avoid this perversion is to fully accept that the Fall is actually the starting point which creates the conditions of Salvation in the first place: there is nothing previous to the Fall from which we fall, the Fall itself creates that from which we fall. Such a position opens up the space for the justification of Evil: if we know that Evil is just a necessary detour on the path towards the final triumph of the Good, then, of course, we are justified in engaging in Evil as the means to achieving the Good. However, there is no Reason in History whose divine plan can justify Evil; the Good that may come out of Evil is only a contingent by-product. We can say that the ultimate result of Nazi Germany and its defeat was the rise of much higher ethical standards of human rights and international justice; however, to claim that this result in any sense 'justifies' Nazism is an obscenity. It is only in this way that we can truly avoid the perverse logic of religious fundamentalism. Among the Christian thinkers, it is – as usual – G. K. Chesterton who was not afraid to explain the consequences of this paradox, locating precisely at this point the break between the Classical world and Christianity:

> The Greeks, the great guides and pioneers of pagan antiquity, started out with the idea of something splendidly obvious and direct; the idea that if man walked straight ahead on the high road of reason and nature, he would come to no harm ... And the case of the Greeks themselves is alone enough to illustrate the strange but certain fatality that attends upon this fallacy. No sooner did the Greeks themselves begin to follow their own noses and their own notion of being natural, than the queerest thing in history seems to have happened to them ... The wisest men in the world set out to be natural; and the most unnatural thing in the world was the very first thing they did. The immediate effect of saluting the sun and the sunny sanity of nature was a perversion spreading like a pestilence. The greatest and even the purest philosophers could not apparently avoid this sort of lunacy. Why? ... When Man goes straight he goes crooked. When he follows his nose he manages somehow to put his nose out of joint, or even to cut off his nose to spite his face; and that in accordance with something much deeper in human nature than nature-worshippers could ever understand. It was the discovery of that deeper thing, humanly speaking, that constituted the conversion to Christianity. There is a bias in a man like the bias on

> a bowl; and Christianity was the discovery of how to correct the bias and therefore hit the mark. There are many who will smile at the saying; but it is profoundly true to say that the glad good news brought by the Gospel was the news of original sin.[28]

The Greeks thus lost their moral compass precisely because they believed in the spontaneous and basic uprightness of a human being, and thus neglected the 'bias' towards Evil you find at the very core of a human being: true Good does not arise when we follow our nature, but when we fight it.[29] The same point was made in Richard Wagner's opera *Parsifal*, whose final message is: 'The wound can be healed only by the spear that smote it' (*Die Wunde schliesst der Speer nur, der sie schlug*). Hegel says the same thing, although with the accent shifted in the opposite direction, when he talks about *Spirit* as the active power which constantly undermines ('negates') and transforms all inert and stable reality: the Spirit is itself the wound it tries to heal, i.e., the wound is self-inflicted. That is to say, what is 'Spirit' at its most elementary? The 'wound' of nature: the spirit of human subjectivity is the power of differentiating, of 'abstracting,' of tearing apart and treating as free-standing what in reality is part of an organic unity. Spirit is nothing but the process of overcoming natural immediacy and organic unity, the process of the elaboration ('mediation') of this immediacy, of withdrawing-into-itself or 'taking off' from it, of alienating itself from it. Spirit's return-to-itself creates the very dimension to which it returns.

Doesn't the Bible say exactly the same thing? The serpent promises Adam and Eve that, by eating the fruit of the tree of knowledge, *they* will become like God; and *after the two do it*, God says: 'Behold, Adam has become like one of us.' (Genesis 3:22) Hegel's comment is: 'So the serpent did not lie, for God confirms what it said.' As Hegel would have it, subjective knowledge is not just the possibility to choose evil or good, 'it is the consideration or the cognition that *makes* people evil, so that consideration and cognition *themselves* are what is evil, and that *therefore* such cognition is what ought not to exist *because it* is the *source* of evil.'[30] Or, even more pointedly, Evil is the gaze itself that perceives Evil everywhere around it: the gaze that sees Evil excludes itself from the social Whole it criticizes, and this exclusion is *itself* the formal characteristic of Evil. And Hegel's point is that the Good emerges as a possibility and duty only through this primordial choice of Evil: we experience the Good when, after choosing Evil, we become aware of the utter inadequacy of our situation. At a more conceptual level of his logic of reflection, Hegel uses the unique term *absoluter Gegenstoss* (recoil, counter-push, counter-thrust, or simply counter-punch) to designate a withdrawal-from which *creates* that from which it withdraws: 'What is thus found only *comes to be* through being *left behind* ... The reflective movement is to be taken as an *absolute recoil* upon itself.'[31] So it is 'only in the return itself' that what we return to emerges at all – it begins to exist or to be perceived as a possibility where before there was no trace of it.

We are not talking here about abstract theoretical points, but about a very concrete historical experience. According to some Indian cultural theorists, the fact that they are compelled to use the English language is a form of cultural colonialism which censors their true identity: 'We have to speak in an imposed foreign language to express our innermost identity, and does this not put us in a position of radical alienation – even our resistance to colonization has to be formulated in the language of the colonizer?' The answer to this is: yes – but this imposition of English (a foreign language) created the very thing which is 'oppressed' by it, i.e., what is oppressed is not the actual pre-colonial India, which has been for ever lost, but the authentic dream of a new universalist democratic India. (Malcolm X was following the same insight when he adopted X as his family name: he was not fighting on behalf of the return to some primordial African roots, but precisely on behalf of an X, an unknown new identity opened up by the very process of slavery which made the African roots for ever lost.) This case shows how the point is not that there is nothing prior to the loss: of course there was something before the loss – in the case of India, a vast and complex tradition – but this lost tradition was a heterogeneous mess that has nothing to do with that to which the later national revival wants to return. This holds for all 'return to origins': when, from the nineteenth century onwards, new nation-states were popping up in Central and Eastern Europe, their return to 'old ethnic roots' generated these very same roots, producing what the Marxist historian Eric Hobsbawm calls 'invented traditions'.

There is a nicely vulgar joke about Christ: the night before he was arrested and crucified, his followers start to worry: Christ was still a virgin, wouldn't it be nice to have him experience a little bit of pleasure before he dies? So they ask Mary Magdalene to go to the tent where Christ is resting and seduce him; Mary says she would gladly do it and goes in, but five minutes later she runs out screaming, terrified and furious.

The followers ask her what went wrong, and she explains: 'I slowly undressed, spread my legs and showed to Christ my pussy; he looked at it and said, "What a terrible wound! It should be healed!" and gently put his palm on it . . .' So beware of people too intent on healing other people's wounds – what if one enjoys one's wound? In exactly the same way, directly healing the wound of colonialism (effectively returning to the pre-colonial reality) would have been a nightmare: if today's Indians were to find themselves in pre-colonial reality, they would undoubtedly utter the same terrified scream as Mary Magdalene.

This, then, is our definition of Event at this stop in our journey: the ultimate Event is the Fall itself, the loss of some primordial unity and harmony which never existed, which is just a retroactive illusion. The surprising fact is that this topic of Fall also resonates outside religious fields, in the most radical version of today's science, quantum cosmology. The question that quantum cosmology is tackling today is: why is there something and not nothing? Science offers here two models: Big Bang and symmetry breaking. The Big Bang theory, currently the predominant theory about the origin of the universe, claims that (our) universe began from an initial point or singularity which has expanded over billions of years to form the universe as we now know it. Singularity means a point or region in space-time in which gravitational forces cause matter to have infinite density, so that the laws of physics are suspended: the quantities that are used to measure the gravitational field become infinite, so that all calculation based on the laws of physics becomes meaningless and the subsequent behaviour of the system cannot be predicted. This suspension of the laws as the key feature of a singularity allows us to use the term also in other contexts – Ray Kurzweil, for example, defined a Technological Singularity as:

> 'a future period during which the pace of technological change will be so rapid, its impact so deep, that human life will be irreversibly transformed. Although neither utopian nor dystopian, this epoch will transform the concepts that we rely on to give meaning to our lives, from our business models to the cycle of human life, including death itself.[32]

For understandable reasons, Catholics see the Big Bang as providing an opening for God: the suspension of the laws of nature at the point of singularity means that this event is not natural; it indicates a direct supernatural intervention, and singularity is thus the scientific name for the moment of creation (Catholics like to point out that the 'father of the Big Bang Theory' was Father Georges Lemaître, a Catholic priest from Belgium, who proposed its first formulation in 1933). When Pope John Paul II received Stephen Hawking, he allegedly told him: 'We are well in agreement, mister astrophysicist: what happens after the big bang is your domain; what happens before is ours . . .' Even if this exchange did not really take place, it makes the right point.

Philosophically, what is perhaps more interesting is the notion of broken symmetry, since it provides an answer to how something emerges out of nothing by way of redefining nothingness itself. The vacuum state or the quantum vacuum is not some absolutely empty void: it contains fleeting electromagnetic waves and particles that pop into and out of existence.

When these (infinitesimally) small fluctuations in energy act on a system which is crossing a critical point, they decide the system's fate by determining which branch of a bifurcation it will take; to an outside observer unaware of the fluctuations (or, 'noise'), the choice will appear arbitrary. The process is called symmetry breaking because such a transition brings the system from a homogenous disorderly state into one of two definite states. The best-known physical example is that of a spherical ball balanced on a (symmetrical) hill: an imperceptibly small disturbance of the ball's position will cause it to quickly roll down the hill into its lowest energy state, so that a perfectly symmetrical situation will collapse into an asymmetrical state. The key point is that this collapse is genuinely contingent: it is not that the causes are so tiny that we cannot perceive them; much more radically, the fluctuations take place at the level of not-fully-existing (pre-ontological) virtual entities which are, in a way, less than nothing. The speculative insight of this notion of broken symmetry resides in the identity between nothingness (void, vacuum) and the infinite wealth of potentialities. In this shadowy space, 'normal' laws of nature are continuously suspended – how? Imagine that you have to take a flight on day X to pick up a fortune the next day, but do not have the money to buy the ticket; but then you discover that the accounting system of the airline is such that if you were to wire the ticket payment within 24 hours of arrival at your destination, no one would ever know it was not paid prior to departure. In a homologous way,

> the energy a particle has can wildly fluctuate so long as this fluctuation is over a short enough time scale. So, just as the accounting system of the airline 'allows' you

> to 'borrow' the money for a plane ticket provided you pay it back quickly enough, quantum mechanics allows a particle to 'borrow' energy so long as it can relinquish it within a time frame determined by Heisenberg's uncertainty principle ... But quantum mechanics forces us to take the analogy one important step further. Imagine someone who is a compulsive borrower and goes from friend to friend asking for money ... Borrow and return, borrow and return – over and over again with unflagging intensity he takes in money only to give it back in short order ... a similar frantic shifting back and forth of energy and momentum is occurring perpetually in the universe of microscopic distance and time intervals.[33]

This is how, even in an empty region of space, a particle emerges out of Nothing, 'borrowing' its energy from the future and paying for it (with its annihilation) before the system notices this borrowing. The whole network can function like this, in a rhythm of borrowing and annihilation, one borrowing from the other, displacing the debt on to the other, postponing the payment of the debt – it is really like the sub-particle domain playing Wall Street games with futures. What this presupposes is a minimal temporal gap between the existence of things in their immediate brute reality, and the registration of this reality in some medium. The most obvious example of this gap is the death of a human being: it is one thing to die in reality, and another for this death to be properly registered, taken into account, by the public authorities – sometimes, the authorities falsely register one of their living subjects as dead, so that the poor citizen has to prove to the state that he is still alive. In France, one can even obtain a document called a *certificat d'existence*, a legal proof that one exists.

The theological implications of this gap between the virtual proto-reality and the fully constituted one are of special interest. Insofar as 'God' is the agent who creates things by way of observing them, the quantum indeterminacy compels us to posit a god who is *omnipotent, but not omniscient*: 'If God collapses the wave functions of large things to reality by His observation, quantum experiments indicate that He is not observing the small.'[34] The ontological cheating with virtual particles (an electron can create a proton and thereby violate the principle of constant energy, on condition that it reabsorbs it before its environs 'take note' of the discrepancy) is a way to cheat God himself, the ultimate agency of taking note of everything that goes on: God himself doesn't control the quantum processes, therein resides the atheist lesson of quantum physics. Einstein was right with his famous claim 'God doesn't cheat' – what he forgot to add is that he himself can be cheated: there are micro-processes (quantum oscillations) that are not registered by the system.

There is a fundamental asymmetry between the two events, the Big Bang and the breaking of symmetry: the Big Bang is the explosion of an infinitely compressed singularity, while broken symmetry is a collapse of an infinite field of potentialities into a determined finite reality. The two events can be opposed in many ways: relativity theory versus quantum cosmology, idealism versus materialism. But the fundamental lesson remains the same, the lesson of radical imbalance: the ultimate Event is the Fall itself, i.e., *things emerge when the equilibrium is destroyed, when something goes astray*. This lesson seems the very opposite of Buddhism, which sees the source of suffering and evil in our excessive attachment to worldly objects, and, consequently, admonishes us to withdraw from our engagements and to adopt a detached attitude as the only way to break out of the vicious circle of suffering. Are things as simple as that? The Japanese Buddhist Sakaguchi Ango (1906–55) criticized Buddhism for its detachment from actual life with all its passions; he proposed 'starting a new life that follows common desires'. However, at the moment when he left the world of Buddhism, Ango 'can be said to have become truly Buddhist. He never wrote positively about Buddhism. In particular, he was extremely vitriolic against anything with pretensions to a Zen-like enlightenment or subdued refinement. Yes, paradoxical as it may seem, his criticism is eminently Buddhist.'[35]

The central notion of Ango was 'fallenness' – he encouraged readers to continue to fall. However, fall – *daraku* – 'does not contain the usual sense of "decadence" ... For Ango, fallenness meant existing in a state of exposure and opening to the other.'[36] In short, authenticity is fallenness itself: we leave behind our false Self not when we keep reality at a distance, but precisely when we totally, without reserve, 'fall' into it, abandon ourselves to it. The illusion of our Self persists precisely insofar as we perceive reality as something 'out there,' outside 'me here'. This notion of a redemptive Fall is, perhaps, the most precious secret of Buddhism. So what can Buddhism tell us about Event? This brings us to the next stop in our journey: Event as the moment of Enlightenment, of getting disentangled from the cobweb of illusory reality and entering the void of Nirvana.

STOP 3

Buddhism Naturalized

When did *the* Event take place? In 1654, James Ussher published in London part two of his monumental *Annals of the Old and New Testaments*. A Protestant bishop in Ireland – a Catholic land if there ever was one – he wanted to demonstrate the superiority of the rational approach over the superstitious 'papists,' so he studied thousands of sources to establish scientifically the exact date of Creation. His conclusive answer was: God created the world at the beginning of the night before 23 October 4004 BC. (One wonders why at the beginning of the night? Why not in the morning, after God had enjoyed a hearty English breakfast to give him strength for the hard work ahead?)[37] Ussher's dating made him a legend, providing the first case of a specifically British tradition which echoes even in Virginia Woolf's *Mr. Bennett and Mrs. Brown* from 1924, where she claims that 'on or about April 1910 human nature changed.' While, of course, agreeing with her, we should maybe propose a new date for *the* Event: our own time, when the ongoing progress in biogenetics such as cloning is effectively changing human nature, disrupting

the conditions of human reproduction and radically

> disconnect[ing] it from the encounter of the two sexes, thus opening the possibility of generalized eugenics, of the fabrication of clones, monsters, or hybrids, which shatters the limits of a species. The limits of the biological real are effectively displaced, and the most secured constraints of what is to be symbolized, life, death, filiation, bodily identity, the difference of the sexes, are rendered friable. Cloning allows us, in principle, to get rid of a partner, and thereby of the other sex, or of the alterity as such: one perpetuates oneself without alteration. There is a historical mutation in this which is at least as radical as the death of the human species made possible by nuclear fission.[38]

Indeed, the neuro-discourse in which a person is equated to his or her brain (or, sometimes, simply his or her DNA) has penetrated all aspects of our lives, from law to politics to literature to medicine to physics.[39] As part of this neuro-revolution, huge military funds are invested in neuro-scientific research; the most conspicuous case is that of the (in)famous American DARPA (Defense Advanced Research Projects Agency), which comprises three strands: narrative analysis; augmented cognition (along the lines of the Iron Man project, etc., to create soldiers with enhanced cognitive capacities); and autonomous robots (aiming to convert a large fraction of the military into a robotic one, which is easier to control, will decrease the economic burden of having military personnel, and will reduce losses in terms of soldiers' lives). Autonomous robot-soldiers can also be used to ruthlessly stop protests and crack down on citizens in cases of civil disobedience. Critical scientists like

Ahmed El Hady made it clear what awaits us at the end of this road:

> The 'educational neuroscience' framework combines with the promotion of 'Expert culture' on a global scale to convert the population into 'empty' individuals indoctrinated with fragmented knowledge, acting locally to solve specific problems dissociated from any collective or global endeavors.
>
> Another scenario is the use of brain control modalities to immediately end any revolutionary uprising. In addition to controlling your brain narratives and autonomous robotic soldiers ... brain control modalities can also include neurotropic drugs that alter the psychological state of the individuals, neurotoxins that can control or stop the activity of the brain, and neuromicrobiological agents that deliver pathogens to the brain thus rendering it dysfunctional.[40]

The basic idea of DARPA is to protect the citizens of the United States from (foreign) bad guys by figuring out how vulnerable some people are to terrorist 'narratives' (oral stories, speeches, propaganda, books, etc.), and then supplanting such narratives with better ones. To put it simply, DARPA endeavours to shape minds with stories. How? Here is the catch: DARPA would like to revolutionize the study of narrative influence by extending it into the neurobiological domain. The standard narrative analysis thus takes an ominous turn: the goal is not to convince the potential terrorist through apt rhetoric or line of argument (or even plain brainwashing), but to directly intervene in his brain to make him change his mind. Ideological struggle is no longer conducted through argument or propaganda, but by means of neurobiology, i.e., by way of regulating neuronal processes in our brain. Again, the catch is: who will decide what narratives are dangerous and, as such, deserve neurological correction?

In 2011, a DARPA-financed project gained some publicity under the headline PARALYSED MAN MOVES ROBOTIC ARM WITH HIS THOUGHTS: 'The nearby robotic hand that Tim Hemmes was controlling with his mind touched his girlfriend Katie Schaffer's outstretched hand. One small touch for Mr. Hemmes; one giant reach for people with disabilities.'[41] This 'miracle' is based on electrocorticography (ECoG), in which an electronic grid is surgically placed against the brain (without penetrating it) and can thus non-intrusively capture brain signals: ECoG picks up an array of brain signals that a computer algorithm can interpret and then move a robotic arm, based on the person's intentions. In the next step, the team plans to make the technology wireless, and to include sensors in the prosthesis that can send signals back to the brain to simulate sensation. It is difficult to miss the joke here. Tech-gnostics are promising us that, by wiring our brains into machines, we will enter a post-human era and return to the angelic state before the Fall: sex will no longer be needed, our minds will communicate directly, while our bodies will be reduced to external instruments produced through cloning and other scientific procedures. However, in the case of Mr Hemmes, science was mobilized to enable a man to touch a woman, his sexual object, the very cause of his Fall according to the Bible. So, what does the prospect of such direct neurobiological interventions mean for our sex lives?

In late 1925, Andrei Platonov – together with Beckett and Kafka one of the three *absolute* writers of the twentieth century – wrote a unique short essay called 'Anti-Sexus'.[42] In it he presents himself only as the translator of a propaganda brochure produced by a big Western company which wants to penetrate the Soviet market. After the translator's introduction, the company's head describes the product, and what then follows are the short comments of well-known public figures (from Mussolini to Gandhi, Henry Ford to Charlie Chaplin, and from J. M. Keynes to Marshal Hindenburg) about the product – a mass-produced masturbatory machine which allows the user to reach a fast and intense orgasm. In this way, humanity can be relieved from the intricacies of sexual love: sexual need loses its uncontrollable character, it no longer involves the time- and energy-consuming process of seduction and becomes something available to anyone in a simple and planned way, thus promising a new era of inner peace. Although 'Anti-Sexus' is obviously a satirical piece, things get complicated the moment we try to determine the precise object of satire. It is usually taken that Chaplin's comment, which is the only negative one and claims that the product will deprive us of the intense and deeply spiritual inter-human contact which characterizes genuine sexual love, stands for the position of Platonov himself, but does it?

• • •

The importance of 'Anti-Sexus' resides in paradoxically bringing together three orientations which are independent from each other and sometimes even antagonistic: the equation of sex with the Fall, which characterizes the Gnostic dualist tradition. Gnosticism claims to possess a direct spiritual insight into our reality which is composed of two opposing forces: Light and Darkness, Good and Evil. The material world of procreation is by definition evil and was created by a lower heavenly creator/demiurge, not by God himself (the sect of *skopcy* whose male members voluntarily castrated themselves deeply impressed Platonov); the biotechnological prospect of total regulation or even abolition of sex; and the commodification of sex in capitalist consumerism. Modern biotechnology provides a new way to realize the old Gnostic dream of getting rid of sex – however, the gadget which does it comes from capitalism and presents itself as the ultimate commodity.

In hindsight, the gadget imagined by Platonov neatly fits the ongoing shift in the predominant libidinal economy, in the course of which the relationship to a human Other is gradually replaced by the captivation of individuals by what Lacan baptized with the neologism *les lathouses*: consumerist object-gadgets which attract the libido with their promise to deliver excessive pleasure, but which effectively reproduce only the lack itself. (The pleasure provided by a plastic sex toy always leaves us hungry for more – the more we use it the more we feel the need to use it again.)

• • •

This is how psychoanalysis approaches the libidinal-subjective impact of new technological inventions: 'technology is a catalizer, it enlarges and enhances something which is already here'[43] – in this case, a fantasmatic virtual fact. And, of course, this realization changes the entire constellation: once a fantasy is realized, once a fantasmatic object directly appears in reality, reality is no longer the same. And, effectively, one finds on today's market a gadget close to what Platonov imagined: the so-called 'Stamina Training Unit,' a masturbatory device which resembles a battery torch (so that, when we carry it around, we are not embarrassed). You put the erect penis into the opening at the top and move the thing up and down till satisfaction's achieved. The product is available in different colours, tightnesses and forms that imitate all three main openings for sexual penetration (mouth, vagina, anus). What one buys here is simply the partial object (erogenous zone) alone, deprived of the embarrassing additional burden of the entire person. While phallic vibrators have been available for a long time, the 'Stamina Training Unit' makes a step further in providing their masculine counterpart.

How are we to cope with this brave new world which undermines the basic premises of our social life and of our innermost self-understanding? The ultimate solution would be, of course, to push a vibrator into the 'Stamina Training Unit,' turn both of them on and leave all the fun to this 'ideal couple,' with us, human subject, reduced to detached observers of the mechanical interplay. And this brings us to Buddhism: if, after achieving Buddhist Enlightenment – the full inner detachment from material reality – we were to engage in the sexual act, would our experience not be strictly homologous to such an observer of the interplay of two sex gadgets? What if the growing popularity of Buddhism is more than just a phenomenon of fashion? Two features that characterize our epoch are the expansion of global capitalism, with its frantic rhythm of self-reproduction, and the key role of science. In both cases, Buddhism imposes itself as the most adequate reaction: the subjective stance most able to contend with global capitalism and the scientific worldview.

Although Buddhism presents itself as the remedy for the stressful tension of capitalist dynamics, allowing us to uncouple and retain inner peace and *Gelassenheit* (self-surrender), it actually functions as capitalism's perfect ideological supplement. One should mention here the well-known topic of 'future shock,' i.e. how, today, people are no longer psychologically able to cope with the dazzling pace of technological development and the social changes that accompany it. Things simply move too fast; before one can accustom oneself to an invention, it is already supplanted by a new one, so that one more and more lacks the most elementary 'cognitive mapping' needed to grasp these developments. The recourse to Taoism or Buddhism offers a way out of this predicament which works better than a desperate escape into old traditions: instead of trying to cope with the accelerating pace of technological progress and social changes, one should rather renounce the very endeavour to retain control over what goes on, rejecting it as the expression of the modern logic of domination. One should, instead, 'let oneself go,' drift along, while retaining an inner distance and indifference towards the mad dance of accelerated progress, a distance based on the insight that all this social and technological upheaval is ultimately just a non-substantial proliferation of semblances which do not really concern the innermost kernel of our being. One is almost tempted to resuscitate here the infamous Marxist cliché of religion as the 'opium of the people'. The 'Western Buddhist' meditative path is arguably the most efficient way for us to fully participate in capitalist dynamics while retaining the appearance of mental sanity. (If the sociologist Max Weber were alive today, he would have definitely written a second, supplementary volume to his founding text, *The Protestant Ethic and the Spirit of Capitalism* [1904], titled *The Taoist Ethic and the Spirit of Global Capitalism*.)

And does the same not hold even more for the disturbing outcome of today's brain sciences? Doesn't here also Buddhism provide the only consistent answer? Brain sciences are telling us that the notion of Self as a free autonomous subject is a mere user's illusion; that there is no Self, there are just objective neuronal processes. The key question here is: how do we as humans relate to this insight? Is it possible not only to think the self-less world as a theoretical model, but to live it? To live as 'being no one'? Philosophers and scientists propose here different answers. Their predominant attitude is to resign themselves to the gap between the scientific view of ourselves and our everyday self-experience as free autonomous agents: although science is telling us that there is no Self with free will, just 'objective' neuronal and biological processes, we will always experience ourselves as Selves – in the same way that, although we know the Earth turns around the Sun, we continue to talk about the Sun rising and going down.

• • •

Some philosophers (such as Jürgen Habermas) claim our self-perception as free and responsible agents is not just a necessary illusion, but a necessary transcendental condition of scientific knowledge. Habermas developed his position in response to a manifesto in which eleven distinguished German neuroscientists claim that our ordinary concept of free will is on the verge of being overthrown by recent advances in neurobiology: 'We stand at the threshold of seeing our image of ourselves considerably shaken in the foreseeable future.'[44] For Habermas, however, the scientific objectification of humans 'presupposes participation in an intersubjectively instituted system of linguistic practices whose normative valence conditions the scientist's cognitive activity'.[45] In short, we should never forget that the scientific image of man as a neurobiological machine is the result of collective scientific practice in which we act as free rational agents.

Finally, there are some brain scientists (like Patricia and Paul Churchland) who claim that we are not biologically wired to our everyday self-understanding as free autonomous Selves: this self-understanding is conditioned by the limited scope of our traditional knowledge, so we can well imagine and strive for a new everyday self-understanding which would be at the level of our emerging scientific image of human beings. Assuming this scientific image in our daily lives would deprive us of some illusions (of freedom and responsibility), but it would at the same time render our social practices less punitive and oppressive. The problem with this view is its implicit naivety: scientists who advocate it somehow presuppose that the autonomous subject is still here, freely deciding on how to change its 'nature'. This brings us back to our starting question: is it possible for a human being to *live* the fact that Self doesn't exist, to experience this fact as a direct state of his or her mind? The positive answer to this question was provided by contemporary German philosopher and brain scientist Thomas Metzinger.[46]

Metzinger concedes that we cannot help experiencing ourselves as 'selves': one can know (in the purely epistemic sense of objective knowledge), that there is such a thing as a substantial Self – with one exception: Buddhist Enlightenment, in which the Self directly, in its innermost self-experience, assumes its own non-being, i.e., it recognizes itself as a 'simulated self,' a representational fiction. Such an enlightened awareness is no longer self-awareness: it is no longer I who experiences myself as the agent of my thoughts; 'my' awareness is the direct awareness of a self-less system, a self-less knowledge. In short, there effectively *is* a link between the position taken by radical brain sciences and the Buddhist idea of *an-atman* (of the Self's inexistence): Buddhism provides a kind of subjective eventalization of scientific cognitivism: the Event which takes place when we fully assume the results of brain sciences is the Event of Enlightenment, the attainment of Nirvana, which liberates us from the constraints of our Self as an autonomous substantial agent. But does this solution work?

Buddhism is concerned with solving the problem of suffering, so its first axiom is: we don't want to suffer.[47] (For a Freudian, this already is problematic and far from self-evident – not only on account of some obscure masochism, but on account of the deep satisfaction brought by a passionate attachment. I am ready to suffer for a political cause; when I am passionately in love, I am ready to submit myself to passion even if I know in advance that it will probably end in catastrophe and that I will suffer when the affair is over. But even at this point of misery, if I am asked, 'Was it worth it? You are a ruin now!' the answer is an unconditional 'Yes! Every inch of it was worth it! I am ready to go through it again!') The source of suffering resides in the unquenchable desire of people for things which, even if they get them, will never satisfy them. The goal of Buddhist practice is liberation from suffering (Enlightenment, Awakening) – everything a Buddhist does is ultimately for the attainment of Enlightenment. Buddhist practice first focuses on a morality that will lead to Enlightenment; however, morality is only the first step on this path. Like any journey, this moral quest must be embarked upon and then doggedly pursued in order to attain the final goal of freedom from suffering: the proper conduct is in itself insufficient, it should be supplemented by the proper awareness.

Buddhist practice thus begins with conduct, with analysing (and changing) the way we act. There are no higher powers (such as gods) that dictate or judge our actions from outside: our acts, as it were, create their own immanent criteria by way of how they fit into their overall context, and how they strengthen or diminish suffering (our own and of all sentient beings). This is what is meant by the notion of karma: we never act in isolation, our acts always leave traces, and these traces – which can be good, bad or indifferent – continue to haunt the agent long after the act is done. Here enters common morality: the first step of Buddhist practice is to train us to identify and gradually get rid of the unwholesome actions which occur at three levels: body, speech and mind. There are three unwholesome actions of the body that are to be avoided (killing, stealing, sexual misconduct), four actions of speech (lying, slander, harsh speech, malicious gossip), and three actions of mind (greed, anger, delusion). When we gradually diminish these unwholesome acts, following the 'middle way' of avoiding extremes, we are close – although not yet ready – to enter Enlightenment, in which we acquire dispassion for objects, and are thus liberated from suffering (*dukkha*) and from the cycle of incessant rebirths (*saṃsāra*). So what happens to our karma when we find ourselves in Nirvana (the Buddhist 'subjective destitution')? Do our acts leave good traces? The Buddhist answer is: no, we find ourselves in Nirvana, our acts leave *no* traces; we are at a distance – *subtracted* – from the Wheel of Desire. But a problem emerges here: if moderate good acts (the elementary morality with which the Buddhist practice begins) help us to get rid of our excessive attachments, is it then not the case that, when we reach Nirvana, we should be able to perform even brutal evil acts in such a way that they leave no traces, because we perform them at a distance? Would not precisely this ability be the sign of recognition of a true bodhisattva? This is not just the result of abstract speculation, but an historical reality: there is a long tradition of Buddhist warriors, from Ancient Tibet to today's Japan and Thailand, who claim that the detached attitude of Enlightenment makes a perfect cold killing machine.[48]

To clarify this crucial point, look at the key moment of the Buddhist path, the reflexive change from the object to the thinker himself: first, we isolate the thing that bothers us, the cause of our suffering; then, we change – not the object, but ourselves, the way we relate to (what appears to us as) the cause of our suffering: 'What was extinguished was only the *false view* of self. What had always been illusory was understood as such. Nothing was changed but the perspective of the observer.'[49] This shift involves great pain; it is not merely a liberation, a step into the incestuous bliss of what Freud called 'oceanic feeling,' but also the violent experience of losing the ground under one's feet, of being deprived of the most familiar ingredient of one's being. This is why the path towards Buddhist Enlightenment begins with focusing on the most elementary feeling of 'injured innocence,' of suffering an injustice without a cause (the preferred topic of narcissistic masochistic thoughts): 'How could she do this to me? I don't deserve to be treated that way.'[50] The next step is then to make the shift to the Ego itself, to the subject of these painful emotions, rendering clear and palpable its own fleeting and irrelevant status – the aggression against the object that causes suffering should be turned against the Self instead. We do not repair the damage: we gain insight into the illusory nature of the damage, of that which should be repaired.

Here, however, we stumble upon a fundamental ambiguity in the Buddhist edifice: is Nirvana, the goal of Buddhist meditation, just this shift in the subject's stance towards reality? Or is the goal the fundamental transformation of reality itself, so that all suffering disappears, so that all living beings are relieved of their suffering? That is to say, is not the effort to enter Nirvana caught between two radically opposed extremes, the minimalist and maximalist one? On the one side, reality remains as it is, nothing changes, it is just fully perceived as what it is, a mere insubstantial flow of phenomena that doesn't really affect the void at the core of our being. On the other side, the goal is to transform reality itself so that there will be no suffering in it, so that all living beings will enter Nirvana.

This key problem returns in different versions, repeating itself in displaced forms: (1) When we reach Enlightenment and liberate ourselves, should we remain there or should we, out of love for suffering humanity, return to help others to liberate themselves? (2) Is it possible to overcome the gap between Enlightenment and ethical activity: 'How does one get from the metaphysical insight that I have no Self, to the ethic of compassion and loving kindness for others, who are also not selves?'[51] Is it also not possible to draw from *an-atman* the opposite conclusion: live fully in the present and pursue all pleasures possible, without caring for others? (3) How are we to distinguish between happiness achieved by hard work, discipline and meditation, and happiness achieved by magic pills (false beliefs, chemical means), if there is no immanent distinction in the quality of happiness? In other words, 'undeserved' happiness is still happiness. (Plus, once we know happiness can be achieved through chemical means, is it not the case that we have to accept that *all* happiness is based on chemical processes, including the ones going on in our brain when we meditate?) So there is really no difference between deserved and non-deserved happiness: in both cases, the underlying process is chemical. In other words, if Enlightenment can be generated through chemical means ('Enlightenment pills'), is it still a true Enlightenment, an authentic spiritual Event?

What these impasses of Buddhism indicate is that it is difficult, if not outright impossible, to get rid of the dimension of subjectivity in the sense of free responsible agency. There is always something false in simply accepting fate, or in treating oneself as an objective entity, part of neurobiological reality. This falsity is made abundantly clear in how Ted Hughes accounts for his betrayal of Sylvia Plath. If, in the story of modern literature, there ever was a person who exemplifies ethical defeat it is Ted Hughes. The true Other Woman, the focus of the Hughes–Plath saga ignored by both camps, is Assia Wevill, a dark-haired Jewish beauty, a Holocaust survivor and Ted's mistress on account of whom he left Sylvia. So this was like leaving a wife and marrying the mad woman in the attic – however, how did she become mad in the first place? In 1969, she killed herself in the same way as Sylvia had (by gassing herself), but killing along with her also Shura, her daughter by Hughes. Why? What drove *her* into this uncanny repetition? *This* was Ted's true ethical betrayal, not Sylvia. Here, his *Birthday Letters*, with its fake mythologizing, turn into an ethically repulsive text, putting the blame on the dark forces of Fate which run our lives, casting Assia as the dark seductress: 'You are the dark force. You are the dark destructive force that destroyed Sylvia.'[52]

. . .

Recall the line from Oscar Wilde's *The Importance of Being Earnest*: 'To lose one parent, may be regarded as a misfortune; to lose both looks like carelessness.' Does the same not go for Ted Hughes? 'To lose one wife through suicide may be regarded as a misfortune; to lose two wives looks like carelessness ...' Hughes' version is one long variation on Valmont's '*ce n'est pas ma faute*' from *Liaisons Dangereuses*: it wasn't me, it was Fate – as Hughes put it; responsibility is 'a figment valid only in a world of lawyers as moralists'.[53] All his babble about the Feminine Goddess, Fate, astrology, etc., is ethically worthless, an exercise in mythologizing whose aim is to put the blame on the Other. At the level of our practical-ethical life, any attempt to simply shed responsibility and conceive oneself as an unfree mechanism gets caught in a double bind of freedom; yes, we are doomed, Fate pulls the strings, every manipulator is in his/her turn manipulated, every free agent who decides his own fate is deluded – but to simply endorse and assume this predicament of helplessness in the face of greater forces is also an illusion, an escapist avoidance of the burden of responsibility.

We cannot escape from the clutches of Fate, but we also cannot escape from the burden of responsibility into Fate. Is this not why psychoanalysis is exemplary of our predicament? Yes, we are decentred, caught in a foreign cobweb, over-determined by unconscious mechanisms; yes, I am 'spoken' more than speaking, the unconscious Other speaks through me, but simply assuming this fact (in the sense of rejecting any responsibility) is also false, a case of self-deception. Psychoanalysis makes me even *more responsible* than traditional morality does; it makes me responsible even for what is beyond my (conscious) control.

What this means is that the dimension of subjectivity (in the sense of free autonomous agency) is irreducible: we cannot get rid of it; it continues to haunt every attempt to overcome it. Modern scientific naturalism and Buddhism effectively complement each other: although they may appear radically opposed (cold scientific rationalism versus the ethereal Buddhist spirituality), they are united in their rejection of the Self as a free responsible agent. But the impasses of these two positions show that the Event each of them stands for – the Event of radical naturalization of humans in brain sciences, the Event of Enlightenment, of entering Nirvana, in Buddhism – ultimately fails: the true Event is the Event of subjectivity itself, illusory as it may be. Our next stop should thus be Western philosophy, which reaches its peak in the thought of subjectivity; what we will endeavour to demonstrate is how the status of subjectivity itself is evental.

STOP 4

The Three Events of Philosophy

There are three (and only three) key philosophers in the history of Western metaphysics: Plato, Descartes and Hegel. Each of them enacted a clear break with the past: nothing remained the same after they entered the scene. Plato broke with pre-Socratic cosmology in search of the inner harmony of the universe, and introduced metaphysical idealism; Descartes broke with the medieval vision of reality as a meaningful hierarchic order and introduced two basic ingredients of philosophical modernity – the notion of infinite and meaningless mechanical material reality, and the principle of subjectivity ('I think therefore I am') as the ultimate foundation of our knowledge; and Hegel broke with traditional metaphysics – idealist or materialist – and introduced the era of radical historicity in which all solid forms, social structures and principles are conceived as results of a contingent historical process.

Each of the three thinkers cast a long shadow on those who followed him, but in a very specific *negative* way. Michel Foucault (1926–84) once said that the entire history of Western philosophy could be defined as the history of rejections of

Plato: even today, Marxists and anti-Communist liberals, existentialists and analytic empiricists, Heideggerians and vitalists are all united in their anti-Platonism. And exactly the same holds for Descartes. He is decried by ecologists, feminists, cognitive brain scientists, Heideggerians (again), pragmatists, the proponents of the 'linguistic turn' in philosophy ... Finally, Hegel is the ultimate *bête noire* of the last two centuries of philosophy, criticized by Marxists, liberals, religious moralists, deconstructionists and Anglo-Saxon empiricists (among others).

Does this exceptional status of Plato, Descartes and Hegel not provide the ultimate proof that, in each case, we are dealing with a philosophical Event in the sense of *a traumatic intrusion of something New which remains unacceptable for the predominant view*? Furthermore, as well as standing for an Event in philosophy, each thinker stands for a moment of madness: the madness of being captivated by an Idea (like falling in love, like Socrates under the spell of his daemon); the madness at the heart of Descartes' *cogito* (what the mystics call the 'night of the world,' the withdrawal from external reality into the abyss of subjectivity); and the madness of Hegel's absolute idealism which pretends to spin the entire wealth of reality out of the self-deployment of the Idea. One can thus say that philosophies which follow Plato, Descartes or Hegel are all attempts to contain/control this excess of madness, to renormalize it, to re-inscribe it into the normal flow of things.

However, the main reason for dealing with these three thinkers lies elsewhere: not only does each of them stand for an Event of thought, but they are also *philosophers of the Event*, i.e., the very focus of each is Event: the event of the shattering encounter of an Idea in Plato; the emergence of a purely evental *cogito*, a crack in the great chain of being, in Descartes; and the Absolute itself – the totality that encompasses everything that exists – as an evental self-deployment, as the result of its own activity, in Hegel.

Connection 4.1 – Truth Hurts

In the textbook version of Plato's idealism, the only true reality is the immutable eternal order of Ideas, while the ever-changing material reality is just its frail shadow. Within such a view, events belong to our unstable material reality; they don't concern the eternal order of Ideas where precisely nothing happens. Is this, however, the only possible reading of Plato? Remember Plato's description of Socrates when he is seized by an Idea: it is as if Socrates is the victim of a hysterical seizure, standing frozen on the spot for hours, oblivious to reality around him – is Plato not describing here an event par excellence, a sudden traumatic encounter with another, supra-sensible dimension which strikes us like lightning and shatters our entire life? For Plato, the first and most elementary form of such an encounter is the experience of love, and it is no wonder that, in his dialogue *Phaedrus*, he compares love to madness, to being possessed – is this not how it is when we find ourselves passionately in love? Is love not a kind of permanent state of exception? All proper balances of our daily life are disturbed, everything we do is coloured by the underlying thought of 'that' – or, as Neil Gaiman, the author of the famous *Sandman* series of graphic novels, wrote in a memorable passage:

> Have you ever been in love? Horrible isn't it? It makes you so vulnerable. It opens your chest and it opens up your heart and it means that someone can get inside you and mess you up. You build up all these defenses, you build up a whole suit of armor, so that nothing can hurt you, then one stupid person, no different from any other stupid person, wanders into your stupid life … You give them a piece of you. They didn't ask for it. They did something dumb one day, like kiss you or smile at you, and then your life isn't your own anymore. Love takes hostages. It gets inside you. It eats you out and leaves you crying in the darkness, so simple a phrase like 'maybe we should be just friends' turns into a glass splinter working its way into your heart. It hurts. Not just in the imagination. Not just in the mind. It's a soul-hurt, a real gets-inside-you-and-rips-you-apart pain. I hate love.[54]

Such a situation is beyond Good and Evil. When we are in love we feel a weird indifference towards our moral obligations with regard to our parents, children, friends – even if we continue to meet them, we do it in a mechanical way, in a condition of 'as if'; everything pales with regard to our passionate attachment. In this sense, falling in love is like the striking light that hit Saul/Paul on the road to Damascus: a kind of religious suspension of the Ethical, to use Kierkegaard's term. An Absolute intervenes which derails the balanced run of our daily affairs: it is not so much that the standard hierarchy of values is inverted – it is much more radical, another dimension enters the scene, a different level of being. French philosopher

Alain Badiou examined the parallel between today's search for a sexual (or marital) partner through the appropriate dating agencies and the ancient procedure of arranged marriages: in both cases, the risk of falling in love is suspended. There is no contingent 'fall' proper, the risk of the 'love encounter' is minimized by prior arrangements which take into account all the material and psychological interests of the concerned parties. Psychologist Robert Epstein pushes this idea to its logical conclusion, providing its missing counterpart: once you choose your appropriate partner, how can you arrange things so that you will both effectively love each other? Such a procedure for choosing a partner relies on self-commodification: through internet dating or marriage agencies, each prospective partner presents themselves as a commodity, listing his or her qualities and providing photos. Within this model, if we marry today, it is more and more in order to re-normalize the violence of falling in love, the violence nicely indicated by the Basque term for falling in love – *maitemindu* – which, literally translated, means 'to be injured by love'. It is also for this reason that finding oneself in the position of the beloved is so violent, even traumatic. Indeed, W. B. Yeats' well-known lines on love describe one of the most claustrophobic constellations that one can imagine:

Had I the heavens' embroidered cloths,
Enwrought with golden and silver light,
The blue and the dim and the dark cloths
Of night and light and the half-light,
I would spread the cloths under your feet:
But I, being poor, have only my dreams;

I have spread my dreams under your feet,
Tread softly because you tread on my dreams.[55]

In short, as the French philosopher and writer Gilles Deleuze (1925–95) put it, '*si vous etes pris dans le rêve de l'autre, vous êtes foutu!*' ('If you're trapped in the dream of the other, you're fucked!') And, of course, we are trapped in the same way in an authentic political engagement. In his *Conflict of Faculties*, written in the mid-1790s, Immanuel Kant addresses a simple but difficult question: is there a true progress in history? (He meant ethical progress in freedom, not just material development.) Kant conceded that actual history is confused and allows for no clear proof: think how the twentieth century brought unprecedented democracy and welfare, but also holocaust and the Gulag. But he nonetheless concluded that, although progress cannot be proven, we can discern signs which indicate that progress is possible. Kant interpreted the French Revolution as such a sign which pointed towards the possibility of freedom. Here, the hitherto unthinkable happened – a whole people fearlessly asserted their freedom and equality. For Kant, even more important than the – often bloody – reality of what went on in the streets of Paris, was the enthusiasm that the events in France gave rise to in the hearts of sympathetic observers all around Europe and even across the world:

> The recent Revolution of a people which is rich in spirit, may well either fail or succeed, accumulate misery and atrocity, it nevertheless arouses in the heart of all spectators (who are not themselves caught up in it) a taking of sides according to desires which border on

> enthusiasm and which, since its very expression was not without danger, can only have been caused by a moral disposition within the human race.[56]

Did we not encounter something of the same order when, in 2011, we followed with enthusiasm the Egyptian uprising in Cairo's Tahrir Square? Whatever our doubts, fears and compromises, for that instant of enthusiasm each of us was free and participating in the universal freedom of humanity. For today's historicist sceptics, such an event remains a confused outcome of social frustrations and illusions, an outburst which will probably lead to an even worse situation than the one against which it reacted. But what these sceptics are blind to is the 'miraculous' nature of the events in Egypt: something happened that few predicted, violating the experts' opinions, as if the uprising was not simply the result of social causes but of the intervention of a foreign agency into history, the agency that we can call, in a Platonic way, the Eternal Idea of freedom, justice and dignity. Such miraculous events can also take the form of a momentary personal experience. Jorge Semprún, a Spanish Communist Party member exiled in France and arrested by the Gestapo in 1943, witnessed the arrival of a truckload of Polish Jews at Buchenwald; they were stacked into the freight train almost two hundred to a car, travelling for days without food and water in the coldest winter of the war. On arrival, all in the carriage had frozen to death except for fifteen children, kept warm by the others in the centre of the bundle of bodies. When the children were emptied from the car the Nazis let their dogs loose on them. Soon only two fleeing children were left:

> The little one began to fall behind, the SS were howling behind them and then the dogs began to howl too, the smell of blood was driving them mad, and then the bigger of the two children slowed his pace to take the hand of the smaller … together they covered a few more yards … till the blows of the clubs felled them and, together they dropped, their faces to the ground, their hands clasped for all eternity.[57]

What should not escape our attention is that the freeze of eternity is embodied in hand as partial object: while the bodies of the two boys perish, the clasped hands persist for all eternity like the smile of the Cheshire cat. One can easily imagine how this scene should be filmed: while the soundtrack renders what goes on in reality (the two children are clubbed to death), the image of their hands clasped freezes, immobilized for eternity – while the sound renders temporary reality, the image renders the eternal Real – and eternity is to be taken here in the strictest Platonic sense. There is, however, one big difference between the experience reported by Semprún and the standard textbook Platonism which cannot but strike the eye: for the standard version, Ideas are the only true substantial reality, while in Semprún's case, we are obviously dealing with a fleeting illusory appearance of eternity. How are we to account for this difference?

In one of Agatha Christie's stories, Hercule Poirot discovers that an ugly nurse is the same beautiful person he met on a trans-Atlantic voyage: she had merely put on a wig and obfuscated her natural beauty. Hastings, Poirot's Watson-like companion, sadly remarks how, if a beautiful woman can make herself appear ugly, then the same can also be done in the opposite direction: what, then, remains in man's infatuation beyond deception? Does this insight into the unreliability of the beloved woman not announce the end of love? Poirot answers: 'No, my friend, it announces the beginning of wisdom.' Such a scepticism, such an awareness of the deceptive nature of feminine beauty, misses the point, which is that feminine beauty is nonetheless absolute, an absolute which appears: no matter how fragile and deceptive this beauty is at the level of substantial reality, what transpires in/through it is an Absolute – there is more truth in the appearance than in what is hidden beneath it.

Therein resides Plato's true insight of which he himself was not fully aware: Ideas are not the hidden reality beneath appearances (and in fact, Plato was well aware that this hidden reality is one of ever-changing corruptive and corrupted matter). Instead, Ideas are nothing more but the very form of their appearance, this form as such. Let us take a mathematical attractor: an ideal form or a set of states, unchanging under the specified dynamics, towards which a variable (moving according to the rules of a dynamic system) evolves over time. The existence of this form is purely virtual: it does not exist in itself, it is nothing more than the shape towards which lines and points tend. However, precisely as such, the virtual is the Real of this field: the immovable focal point around which all elements circulate – one should give here to the term 'form' its full Platonic weight, since we are dealing with an 'eternal' Idea in which reality imperfectly participates.

We can now measure the true dimension of Plato's philosophical revolution, so radical that it was misinterpreted by

Plato himself. Plato began by asserting the gap between the spatio-temporal order of reality in its eternal movement of generation and corruption, and the eternal order of Ideas, i.e., the notion that empirical reality can participate in an eternal Idea, that an eternal Idea can shine through it, appear in it (i.e., the individual material table in front of me 'participates' in the Idea of Table; it is its copy). Where Plato got it wrong is in his ontologization of Ideas: he presumed that Ideas form another even more substantial and stable order of true reality than our ordinary material reality. What Plato was not ready (or, rather, able) to accept was the thoroughly virtual, immaterial (or, rather, insubstantial) *evental* status of Ideas: Ideas are something that momentarily appear on the surface of things. Recall the old Catholic strategy to guard men against the temptations of the flesh: when you see in front of you a voluptuous feminine body, imagine how it will look in a couple of decades – the wrinkled skin and sagging breasts (or, even better, imagine what lurks now already beneath the skin: raw flesh and bones, inner fluids, half-digested food and excrements). The same advice had been given by Marcus Aurelius in his *Meditations*, where he wrote apropos making love:

> something rubbing against your penis, a brief seizure and a little cloudy liquid. Perceptions like that – latching onto things and piercing through them, so we see what they really are. That's what we need to do all the time – all through our lives when things lay claim to our trust – to lay them bare and see how pointless they are, to strip away the legend that encrusts them.[58]

Far from enacting a return to the Real destined to break the imaginary spell of the body, such a procedure equals the *escape from the Real*, the Real which announces itself in the seductive appearance of the naked body. That is to say, in the opposition between the spectral appearance of the sexualized body and the repulsive body in decay, it is the spectral appearance which is the Real, and the decaying body which is reality – we take recourse to the decaying body in order to avoid the deadly fascination of the Real which threatens to draw us into its vortex.

In contemporary art we often encounter brutal attempts to 'return to the real,' to remind the spectator (or reader) that he is perceiving a fiction, to awaken him from the sweet dream. This gesture has two main forms which, although opposed, amount to the same. In literature or cinema, there are self-reflexive reminders that what we are watching is a mere fiction – such as the actors on screen addressing us directly as spectators, thus ruining the illusion of the narrative fiction, or the writer directly intervening into the narrative through ironic comments. In theatre, there are occasional brutal events which awaken us to the reality of the stage (such as, for example, slaughtering a chicken onstage). Instead of reading these gestures as attempts to break the spell of illusions and confront us with the bare Real, one should rather denounce them for what they are: the exact opposite of what they claim to be – *escapes from the Real*, desperate attempts to avoid the Real that transpires in (or through) the illusion itself.

This is why – if we return for the last time to love – love has nothing whatsoever to do with an escape into an idealized Romantic universe in which all concrete social differences magically disappear. To refer to Kierkegaard again, 'love believes everything – and yet is never to be deceived'[59] – in contrast to the mistrust which believes nothing and is nevertheless thoroughly deceived. The person who mistrusts others is, paradoxically, in his very cynical disbelief, the victim of the most radical self-deception: as Lacan would have put it, *les non-dupes errent* – the cynic misses the actuality of the appearance itself, however fleeting, fragile and elusive it is, while the true believer believes in appearances, in the magic dimension that 'shines through' an appearance: he sees Goodness in the other where the other himself is not aware of it. Appearance and actuality are here no longer opposed: precisely in trusting appearances, a loving person sees the other the way she effectively is, and loves her for her very foibles, not despite them. With regard to this point, the Oriental notion of the Absolute Void-Substance-Ground beneath the fragile, deceptive appearances that constitute our reality is to be opposed to the notion that it is the ordinary reality that is hard, inert and there, and it is the Absolute that is thoroughly fragile and fleeting. That is to say, what *is* the Absolute? Something that appears to us in fleeting experiences, say, through the gentle smile of a beautiful woman, or even through the warm caring smile of a person who otherwise may seem ugly and rude – in such miraculous, but *extremely fragile* moments, another dimension transpires through our reality. As such, the Absolute is easily corroded; it all too easily slips through our fingers, and must be treated as carefully as a butterfly. In short, the

Absolute is a pure Event, something that just occurs – it disappears before it even fully appears.

Connection 4.2 – The Evental Self

In one of the most disturbing episodes of the TV series *Alfred Hitchcock Presents*, 'The Glass Eye,' Jessica Tandy plays a lone woman who falls for a handsome ventriloquist, Max Collodi. When she gathers the courage to approach him alone in his quarters, she declares her love for him and steps forward to embrace him, only to find that she is holding in her hands a wooden dummy's head. After she withdraws in horror, the 'dummy' stands up and pulls off its mask, and we see the face of a sad old dwarf, who jumps on the table, desperately asking the woman to go away; the ventriloquist is in fact the dummy, while the hideous dummy is the actual ventriloquist. It is the detachable 'dead' organ, the partial object, which is effectively alive, and whose dead puppet is the 'real' person: the 'real' person is merely alive, a survival machine, a 'human animal,' while the actual speaking subject dwells in the apparently 'dead' supplement. In other words, when a human being speaks, it is not this concrete bodily presence which speaks but a spectral entity in it, a 'ghost in the machine' more real than the bodily reality of the person in question. This violent reversal of the usual relationship between the bodily substance and its soul is what Descartes enacts with his notion of *cogito*: the thinking subject is not the soul which is present within the body, but an alien intruder, a homunculus which speaks through it. It is because of this violent reversal that Descartes was able to openly assert the evental (non-substantial) status of his basic principle: the Cartesian *cogito* is not the substantial form of a body, it rather designates the pure process of objectless thinking – 'I think, therefore I am.'[60]

What one should always bear in mind when talking about *cogito*, about the reduction of a human point to the abyssal point of thinking without any external object, is that we are not dealing here with silly and extreme logical games ('imagine that you alone exist …'), but with the description of a very precise existential experience of the radical self-withdrawal, of suspending the existence of all reality around me to a vanishing illusion, which is well-known in psychoanalysis (as psychotic withdrawal) as well as in religious mysticism (under the name of so-called 'night of the world'). After Descartes, this idea was deployed in the basic insight of Friedrich Wilhelm Joseph Schelling (1775–1854), the great German idealist according to whom, prior to its assertion as the medium of the rational Word, the subject is the 'infinite lack of being' – '*unendliche Mangel an Sein*' – the violent gesture of contraction that negates every being outside itself. This idea also forms the core of Hegel's notion of madness: when Hegel determines madness to be a withdrawal from the actual world, the closing of the soul into itself, its 'contraction,' the cutting-off of its links with external reality, he all too quickly conceives of this withdrawal as a 'regression' to the level of the 'animal soul' still embedded in its natural environs and determined by the rhythm of nature (night and day, the seasons, etc.). However, doesn't this withdrawal, on the contrary, designate the severing of the links with the *Umwelt,* or environment, the end of the subject's immersion into its immediate natural environs, and is it, as such, not the founding gesture of 'humanization'? Was this withdrawal-into-self not accomplished by Descartes in his universal doubt and reduction to *cogito,* which also involves a passage through the moment of radical madness? In a fragment from his *Jenaer Realphilosophie*, Hegel uses the mystical term 'night of the world' to characterize this experience of pure Self, of the contraction-into-self of the subject which involves the eclipse of (constituted) reality:

> The human being is this night, this empty nothing, that contains everything in its simplicity – an unending wealth of many representations, images, of which none belongs to him – or which are not present. This night, the inner of nature, that exists here – pure self – in phantasmagorical representations, is night all around it, in which here shoots a bloody head – there another white ghastly apparition, suddenly here before it, and just so disappears. One catches sight of this night when one looks human beings in the eye – into a night that becomes awful.[61]

The symbolic order, the universe of the Word, *logos*, can only emerge from the experience of this abyss. As Hegel puts it, this inwardness of the pure self 'must enter also into existence, become an object, oppose itself to this innerness to be external; return to being. This is language as name-giving power ... Through the name the object as individual entity is born out of the I.'[62] What we must be careful not to miss here is how Hegel's break with the prevailing Enlightenment tradition can be discerned in the reversal of the very metaphor for the subject: the subject is no longer the Light of *Reason* opposed to the non-transparent, impenetrable Stuff (of Nature, Tradition, etc.); his very kernel, the gesture which opens up the space for the Light of Logos, is absolute negativity, the 'night of the world,' the point of utter madness in which fantastic apparitions of 'partial objects' appear all around. Consequently, there is no subjectivity without this gesture of withdrawal – which is why Hegel is fully justified in inverting the standard question of how the fall/regression into madness is possible: the true question is rather how the subject is able to climb out of madness and to reach 'normalcy'. That is to say, the withdrawal-into-self, the cutting-off of the links to the environs, is followed by the construction of a symbolic universe which the subject projects on to reality as a kind of substitute-formation, destined to recompense us for the loss of the immediate, pre-symbolic real. In short, the ontological necessity of 'madness' resides in the fact that it is not possible to pass directly from the purely 'animal soul,' immersed in its natural environs, to 'normal' subjectivity dwelling in its symbolic virtual environs: the 'vanishing mediator' between the two is the 'mad' gesture of radical withdrawal from reality, which opens up the space for its symbolic (re)constitution.

The true point of 'madness' is thus not the pure excess of the 'night of the world,' but the madness of the passage to the Symbolic itself, of imposing a symbolic order on to the chaos of the Real. (Freud, in his analysis of the paranoiac judge Daniel Paul Schreber, points out how the paranoiac 'system' is not madness, but a desperate attempt to *escape* madness – the disintegration of the symbolic universe – through an ersatz universe of meaning.[63]) If madness is constitutive, then *every* system of meaning is minimally paranoiac, 'mad'. Recall Brecht's slogan: 'What is the robbing of a bank compared to the founding of a new bank?' In the same way, we should say: what is the mere madness caused by the loss of reason compared to the madness of reason itself?

No wonder, then, that we encounter the Cartesian *cogito* at the very core of what is today emerging as the predominant form of pathology, the so-called post-traumatic subject. Our socio-political reality imposes multiple versions of external intrusions, traumas, which are just that – meaningless, brutal interruptions that destroy the symbolic texture of the subject's identity. First, there is external physical violence: terror attacks like 9/11, the U.S. 'shock and awe' bombing of Iraq, street violence, rapes, etc., but also natural catastrophes such as earthquakes, tsunamis, and so on. Then there is the 'irrational' (meaningless) destruction of the material base of our inner reality: brain-tumours, Alzheimer's disease, organic cerebral lesions, etc., which can utterly change – destroy, even – the victim's personality. Finally, there are the destructive effects of socio-symbolic violence through social exclusion, etc. Most of these forms of violence have, of course, been known for centuries, some even from the very prehistory of humanity. What is new today is that, since we live in a 'disenchanted' post-religious era, they are more directly experienced as meaningless intrusions of the real, and, for this very reason, although utterly different in nature, they appear as belonging to the same series and produce the same effect. (It is a historical fact that rape was categorized as trauma only in the twentieth century.)

A post-traumatic subject is thus a victim who, as it were, survives its own death: all different forms of traumatic encounters, independent of their specific nature (social, natural, biological, symbolic), lead to the same result: a new subject emerges which survives the death (erasure) of its symbolic identity. There is no continuity between this new post-traumatic subject (the victim of Alzheimer's, say) and its old identity: after the shock, literally a new subject emerges. Its features are well-known from numerous descriptions: a lack of emotional engagement, profound indifference and detachment; it is a subject who is no longer 'in-the-world' in the Heideggerian sense of engaged embodied existence. This subject *lives death as a form of life*.

The properly philosophical dimension of the study of the post-traumatic subject resides in this recognition that what appears as the brutal destruction of the subject's very (narrative) substantial identity is the moment of its birth. The post-traumatic autistic subject is 'living proof' that the subject cannot be identified (or does not fully overlap) with 'stories it is telling itself about itself,' with the narrative symbolic texture of its life: when we take all this away, something (or, rather, *nothing*, but a *form* of nothing) remains, and this something is the pure subject. We should thus also apply to the post-traumatic subject the Freudian notion that a violent intrusion of the real counts as trauma only insofar as a previous trauma resonates in it – *in this case, the previous trauma is that of the birth of subjectivity itself*: a subject emerges when a living individual is deprived of its substantial content, and this constitutive trauma is repeated in the present traumatic experience. This is what Lacan aims at with his claim that the Freudian subject is none other than the Cartesian *cogito*: the *cogito* is not an 'abstraction' from the reality of living, actual individuals with the wealth of their properties, emotions, abilities and relations; it is, on the contrary, this 'wealth of personality' which functions as Lacan's imaginary 'stuff of the I'; the *cogito* is, on the contrary, a very real 'abstraction,' an 'abstraction' which functions as a concrete subjective attitude. The post-traumatic subject, the subject reduced to a substance-less empty form of subjectivity, is the historical 'realization' of *cogito* – recall that, for Descartes, *cogito* is the zero-point of the overlapping of thinking and being at which the subject in a way neither 'is' (he is deprived of all positive substantial content) nor 'thinks' (his thinking is reduced to the empty tautology of thinking that it thinks).

Thus when the contemporary French Hegelian philosopher Catherine Malabou claims that the post-traumatic subject cannot be accounted for in the Freudian terms of the repetition of a past trauma (since the traumatic shock erases all the traces of the past), she remains all too fixed on the traumatic content and forgets to include into the series of past traumatic memories the very erasure of the substantial content, the very subtraction of the empty form from its content.[64] In other words, precisely insofar as it erases the entire substantial content, the traumatic shock *repeats* the past, i.e., the past traumatic loss of substance which is constitutive of the very dimension of subjectivity. *What is repeated here is not some ancient content, but the very gesture of erasing all substantial content.* This is why, when one submits a human subject to a traumatic intrusion, the outcome is the empty form of the 'living-dead' subject, but when one does the same to an animal, the result is simply total devastation: what remains after the violent traumatic intrusion on to a human subject which erases all its substantial content is the pure form of subjectivity, the form which already must have been there.

To put it in yet another way, the subject is the ultimate case of what Freud described as the experience of 'feminine castration' which grounds fetishism: the experience of encountering nothing where we expected to see something (penis). If the fundamental philosophical question is 'why is there something rather than nothing?', the question raised by the subject is 'why is there nothing where there should be something?' The latest form of this surprise occurs in brain sciences: when one looks for the 'material substance' of consciousness, one finds that 'there is nobody home' there – just the inert presence of a piece of meat called 'brain'. So where is the subject here? Nowhere. It is neither the self-acquaintance of awareness, nor, of course, the raw presence of brain matter. When one looks an autistic subject in the eye, one also has the feeling that 'there is nobody home' – but, in contrast to the raw presence of a dead object like brain, one expects someone/something there because the open space for this someone is there. This is subject at its zero-level, like an empty house where 'nobody is home'.

> [T]o kill in cold blood, to 'explode oneself,' as one is used to say, to organize terror, to give to terror the face

> of a chance event emptied of sense: is it really still possible to explain these phenomena by way of evoking the couple of sadism and masochism? Do we not see that their source is elsewhere, not in the transformations of love in[to] hate, or of hate into indifference to hate, namely in a beyond of the pleasure principle endowed with its own plasticity which it is time to conceptualize?[65]

If one wants to get an idea of *cogito* at its purest, its 'degree zero,' one has to take a look at such 'autistic' subjects – a regard which is very painful and disturbing. This is why we resist so adamantly the spectre of *cogito*.

Connection 4.3 – *La vérité surgit de la méprise**

This connection is the properly 'Hegelian' one – which is why Hegel, the philosopher who made the most radical attempt to think the abyss of madness at the core of subjectivity, is also the philosopher who brought to its 'mad' climax the philosophical System as the totality of meaning. This is why, for very good reasons, 'Hegel' stands in the eyes of common sense for the moment at which philosophy gets mad and explodes into a crazy pretence at 'absolute knowledge'. However, Hegel's point here is a much more refined one: not that everything is madness, but that 'normality,' the reign of reason, is a

* Truth arises out of error.

self-assimilation of madness, in the same way that the rule of law is the self-assimilation of crime. In G. K. Chesterton's religious thriller *The Man Who Was Thursday*, a mysterious chief of a super-secret Scotland Yard department is convinced that 'a purely intellectual conspiracy would soon threaten the very existence of civilization':

> He is certain that the scientific and artistic worlds are silently bound in a crusade against the Family and the State. He has, therefore, formed a special corps of policemen, policemen who are also philosophers. It is their business to watch the beginnings of this conspiracy, not merely in a criminal but in a controversial sense ... The work of the philosophical policeman ... is at once bolder and more subtle than that of the ordinary detective. The ordinary detective goes to pot-houses to arrest thieves; we go to artistic tea-parties to detect pessimists. The ordinary detective discovers from a ledger or a diary that a crime has been committed. We discover from a book of sonnets that a crime will be committed. We have to trace the origin of those dreadful thoughts that drive men on at last to intellectual fanaticism and intellectual crime.[66]

In a slightly changed version of this idea, actual political crime would be called 'totalitarianism' and the philosophical crime condensed into the notion of 'totality'. A straight road leads from the philosophical notion of totality to political totalitarianism, and the task of the 'philosophical police' is to discover from a book of Plato's dialogues or a treatise on social contract by Rousseau that a political crime will be committed. The ordinary political policeman goes to secret meetings to arrest revolutionaries; the philosophical policeman goes to philosophical symposia to detect proponents of totality. The ordinary anti-terrorist policeman tries to detect those preparing to blow up buildings and bridges; the philosophical policeman tries to detect those about to deconstruct the religious and moral foundation of our societies.

This provocative analysis demonstrates the limitation of Chesterton – his not being Hegelian enough. What he doesn't get is that *universal(ized) crime is no longer a crime – it sublates (negates or overcomes) itself as crime and turns from transgression into a new order*. He is right to claim that, compared to the 'entirely lawless' philosopher, burglars, bigamists, murderers even, are essentially moral: a thief is a 'conditionally good man,' he doesn't deny property as such, he just wants more of it for himself and is then quite ready to respect it. However, the conclusion to be drawn from this is that crime as such is 'essentially moral,' that it wants just a particular illegal reordering of the global moral order which should itself remain. And, in a truly Hegelian spirit, one should bring this proposition (of the 'essential morality' of the crime) to its immanent reversal: not only is crime 'essentially moral' (in Hegelese: an inherent moment of the deployment of the inner antagonisms and 'contradictions' of the very notion of moral order, not something that disturbs moral order from outside, as an accidental intrusion), but morality itself is essentially criminal – again, not only in the sense that the universal moral order necessarily 'negates itself' in particular crimes, but, more radically, in the sense that the way morality (in the case of theft, property) asserts itself is already in itself a crime – 'property *is* theft,' as they used to say in the nineteenth century. That is to say, one should pass from theft as a particular criminal violation of the universal form of property to this form itself as a criminal violation. What Chesterton fails to perceive is that the 'universalized crime' that he projects into 'lawless modern philosophy' and its political equivalent, the 'anarchist' movement that aims to destroy the totality of civilized life, *already exists* in the guise of the existing rule of law, so that the antagonism between Law and Crime reveals itself to be assimilated into crime: the antagonism between universal and particular crime.

It is in this sense that Chesterton asserted the truly subversive, revolutionary even, character of orthodoxy – in his famous 'Defence of Detective Stories,' he remarks how the detective story 'keeps in some sense before the mind the fact that civilization itself is the most sensational of departures and the most romantic of rebellions ... The police romance is based on the fact that morality is the most dark and daring of conspiracies.'[67] Therein resides the elementary matrix of the Hegelian dialectical process here: the external opposition (between Law and its criminal transgression) is transformed into the opposition, internal to the transgression itself, between particular transgressions and the absolute transgression which appears as its opposite, as the universal Law. This point was clearly made by none other than Richard Wagner who, in his draft of the play *Jesus of Nazareth*, written somewhere between late 1848 and early 1849, attributes to Jesus a series of alternate supplementations to the Commandments:

> The commandment saith: Thou shalt not commit adultery! But I say unto you: Ye shall not marry without

> love. A marriage without love is broken as soon as entered into, and who so hath wooed without love, already hath broken the wedding. If ye follow my commandment, how can ye ever break it, since it bids you to do what your own heart and soul desire? – But where ye marry without love, ye bind yourselves at variance with God's love, and in your wedding ye sin against God; and this sin avengeth itself by your striving next against the law of man, in that ye break the marriage-vow.[68]

The true adultery is not to copulate outside marriage, but to copulate in marriage without love: the simple adultery just violates the Law from outside, while marriage without love destroys it from within, turning the letter of the Law against its spirit. To paraphrase Brecht: what is a simple adultery compared to (the adultery that is a loveless) marriage! It is not by chance that Wagner's underlying formula 'marriage is adultery' recalls the anarchist Pierre-Joseph Proudhon's motto 'property is theft' – in the stormy revolutionary times of 1848, Wagner was not only a Feuerbachian celebrating sexual love,[69] but also a Proudhonian revolutionary demanding the abolition of private property; so no wonder that, a little later in the play, Wagner attributes to Jesus a Proudhonian supplement to 'Thou shalt not steal!':

> This also is a good law: Thou shalt not steal, nor covet another man's goods. Who goeth against it, sinneth: but I preserve you from that sin, inasmuch as I teach you: Love thy neighbour as thyself; which also meaneth: Lay not up for thyself treasures, whereby thou stealest from thy neighbour and makest him to starve:

> for when thou hast thy goods safeguarded by the law of man, thou provokest thy neighbour to sin against the law.[70]

This shift is the shift from the *distortion of a notion* to a *distortion constitutive of this notion*: the shift from theft as a distortion ('negation,' violation) of property to the dimension of theft inscribed into the very notion of property (nobody has the right to fully own the means of production, their nature is inherently collective so every claim that 'this is mine' is illegitimate). As we have just seen, the same goes for crime and Law, for the passage from crime as the distortion ('negation') of the law to crime as sustaining law itself, i.e., to the idea of the Law itself as universalized crime. One should note how the encompassing unity of the two opposed terms (property and theft, law and crime) is the 'lowest,' 'transgressive' one: it is not crime which is a moment of law's self-assimilation (or theft which is a moment of property's self-assimilation); the opposition of crime and law is inherent to crime, law is a subspecies of crime – crime's self-relating negation (in the same way that property is theft's self-relating negation).

It is only against this background that we can grasp what Hegel intended with his notion of 'absolute knowing' – the formula here is: take away the illusion and you lose the truth itself. A truth needs time to make a journey through illusions to form itself. One should put Hegel back into the series of Plato–Descartes–Hegel, corresponding to the triad of Objective–Subjective–Absolute: Plato's Ideas are objective,

Truth embodied; the Cartesian subject stands for the unconditional certainty of my subjective self-awareness. And Hegel, what does he add? If 'subjective' is what is relative to our subjective limitation, and if 'objective' is the way things really are, what does 'absolute' add to it? Hegel's answer: the 'absolute' does add some deeper, more substantial, dimension – it includes (subjective) illusion into (objective) truth itself. The 'absolute' standpoint makes us see how reality includes fiction (or fantasy), how the right choice only emerges after the wrong one. Hegel thus enjoins us to turn around the entire history of philosophy, which constitutes a series of efforts to clearly differentiate *doxa* (popular opinion) from true knowledge: for Hegel, *doxa* is a constitutive part of knowledge, and this is what makes truth temporal and evental. This evental character of truth involves a logical paradox deployed by Jean-Pierre Dupuy, a contemporary French theorist of rationality and catastrophes, in his admirable text on Hitchcock's *Vertigo*:

> An object possesses a property x until the time t; after t, it is not only that the object no longer has the property x; it is that it is not true that it possessed x at any time. The truth-value of the proposition 'the object O has the property x at the moment t' therefore depends on the moment when this proposition is enunciated.[71]

One should note here the precise formulation: it is not that the truth-value of the proposition 'the object O has the property x' depends on the time to which this proposition refers: even when this time is specified, *the truth-value depends on the time when the proposition itself is enounced*. Or, to quote the title of Dupuy's text, 'When I'll die, nothing of our love will ever have existed.' Think about marriage and divorce: the most intelligent argument for the right to divorce (proposed, among others, by none other than the young Marx) does not refer to common vulgarities in the style of 'like all things, love attachments are also not eternal, they change in the course of time,' etc.; it rather concedes that indissolvability is in the very notion of marriage. The conclusion is that divorce always has a retroactive scope: it does not only mean that marriage is now annulled, but something much more radical – a marriage should be annulled because *it never was a true marriage*. (The same holds for Soviet Communism: it is clearly insufficient to say that, in the years of Brezhnev it 'stagnated,' it 'exhausted its potentials, no longer fitting new times'; what its miserable end demonstrates is that it was a historical deadlock *from its very beginning*.)

This paradox provides a clue for the twists and turns of the Hegelian dialectical process. Let us take Hegel's critique of the Jacobin revolutionary Terror as an exercise in abstract negativity of the absolute freedom which cannot stabilize itself in a concrete social order of freedom, and thus has to end in the fury of self-destruction. However, one should bear in mind that, insofar as we are dealing here with a historical choice (between the 'French' way of remaining within the Catholic social order and thus being obliged to engage in the self-destructive revolutionary Terror, and the 'German' way of Reformation), this choice involves exactly the same elementary dialectical par adox as the one – also from *The Phenomenology of Spirit*

(1807) – between the two readings of 'the Spirit is a bone' which Hegel illustrates by the phallic metaphor (phallus as the organ of insemination or phallus as the organ of urination): Hegel's point is *not* that, in contrast to the vulgar empiricist mind which sees only urination, the proper speculative attitude has to choose insemination. The paradox is that the direct choice of insemination is the infallible way to miss it: it is not possible to choose directly the 'true meaning,' i.e., one *has* to begin by making the 'wrong' choice (of urination); the true speculative meaning emerges only through the repeated reading, as the after-effect (or by-product) of the first, 'wrong' reading. And the same goes for social life in which the direct choice of the 'concrete universality' of a particular ethical life-world can only end in a regression to pre-modern organic society that denies the infinite right of subjectivity as the fundamental feature of modernity. Since the subject-citizen of a modern state can no longer accept his immersion in some particular social role that confers on him a fixed place within the organic social Whole, the only way to the rational totality of the modern State leads through revolutionary Terror: one should ruthlessly tear up the constraints of the pre-modern organic 'concrete universality,' and fully assert the infinite right of subjectivity in its abstract negativity. In other words, the point of Hegel's analysis of the revolutionary Terror is not the rather obvious insight into how the revolutionary project involved the unilateral direct assertion of abstract Universal Reason, and was as such doomed to perish in self-destructive fury, since it was unable to organize the transposition of its revolutionary energy into a concrete stable and differentiated social order; Hegel's point is, rather, the enigma of why, in spite of the fact that revolutionary Terror was a historical deadlock, we have to pass through it in order to arrive at the modern rational State.

Take the paradox of the process of apologizing: if I hurt someone with a rude remark, the proper thing for me to do is to offer him a sincere apology, and the proper thing for him to do is to say something like, 'Thanks, I appreciate it, but I wasn't offended. I knew you didn't mean it, so you really owe me no apology!' The point is, of course, that, although the final result is that no apology is needed, one has to go through the entire process of offering it: 'you owe me no apology' can only be said after I *do* offer an apology, so that although formally 'nothing happens' – the offer of apology is proclaimed unnecessary – there is a gain at the end of the process (perhaps, even, the friendship is saved). The dialectical process is thus more refined than it may appear. The standard notion is that, in it, one can only arrive at the final truth through the path of errors, so these errors are not simply discarded, but 'sublated' in the final truth, preserved in it as its moments. What this standard notion misses is how the errors are 'sublated' (negated-preserved-elevated) *precisely as superfluous*.

How is this circle of changing the past possible without recourse to travel back in time? The solution was proposed by the French philosopher Henri Bergson (1859–1941): of course one cannot change the past reality/actuality, but what one can change is the virtual dimension of the past – when something radically New emerges, this New retroactively creates its own possibility, its own causes/conditions.[72] A potentiality can be inserted into (or withdrawn from) past reality. Falling in love changes the past: it is as if I *always-already* loved you, our love was destined, the 'answer of the real'. My present love causes the past which gave birth to it. In Hitchcock's *Vertigo*, it is the opposite that occurs: the past is changed so that it loses the '*objet a*' – Lacan's term for the unattainable object of desire. What Scottie first experiences in *Vertigo* is the *loss* of Madeleine, his fatal love; when he recreates Madeleine in Judy and then finds out that the Madeleine he knew already was Judy pretending to be Madeleine, what he discovers is not simply that Judy is a fake (he knows that she is not the true Madeleine, since he recreated a copy of Madeleine out of her), but that, because she is *not* a fake – she *is* Madeleine, Madeleine *herself* was already a fake – *objet a* disintegrates, the very loss is lost, we get a 'negation of negation'. Scottie's discovery *changes the past*, deprives the lost object of *objet a*. The same temporal paradox characterizes all events proper, including the political ones – the German revolutionary Rosa Luxemburg was well aware of it when, in her polemic against the socialist Eduard Bernstein, she provides two arguments against the revisionist fear that the proletariat will take power prematurely, before the circumstances are ripe:

> The socialist transformation supposes a long and stubborn struggle, in the course of which, it is quite probable the proletariat will be repulsed more than once so that for the first time, from the viewpoint of the final outcome of the struggle, it will have necessarily come

> to power, too early … it will be impossible to avoid the 'premature' conquest of State power by the proletariat precisely because these 'premature' attacks of the proletariat constitute a factor and indeed a very important factor, creating the political conditions of the final victory. In the course of the political crisis accompanying its seizure of power, in the course of the long and stubborn struggles, the proletariat will acquire the degree of political maturity permitting it to obtain in time a definitive victory of the revolution … Since the proletariat is not in the position to seize power in any other way than 'prematurely,' since the proletariat is absolutely obliged to seize power once or several times 'too early' before it can maintain itself in power for good, the objection to the 'premature' conquest of power is at bottom nothing more than a *general opposition to the aspiration of the proletariat to possess itself of State power*.[73]

There is no meta-language: no outside-position from which the agent can calculate how many 'premature' attempts are needed to get at the right moment. Why? Because this is a case of truth which arises out of misrecognition (*la vérité surgit de la méprise*, as Lacan put it), where the 'premature' attempts transform the very space/measure of temporality: the subject 'jumps ahead' and takes a risk in making a move before its conditions are fully met.[74] The subject's engagement in the symbolic order coils the linear flow of time in both directions: it involves precipitation as well as retroactivity (things retroactively become what they are; the identity of a thing only emerges when the thing is in delay with regard to itself) – in short, every act is by definition too early and, simultaneously, too late. One has to know to wait, not to lose one's nerve: if one acts too fast, the act turns into a *passage à l'acte*, a violent forward-escape to avoid the deadlock. If one misses the moment and acts too late, the act loses its quality of an event, of a radical intervention as a consequence of which 'nothing remains the way it was,' and becomes just a local change within the order of being, part of the normal flow of things. The problem is, of course, that an act always occurs simultaneously too fast (the conditions are never fully ripe, one has to succumb to the urgency to intervene, there is never enough time to wait, enough time for strategic calculations, the act has to anticipate its certainty and risk that it will retroactively establish its own conditions) and too late (the very urgency of the act signals that we come too late, that we always should have already acted; every act is a reaction to circumstances which arose because we were too late to act). In short, *there is no right moment to act* – if we wait for the right moment, the act is reduced to an occurrence in the order of being.

It is because of this temporal complication that, in Hegel, everything becomes evental: a thing is the result of the process (event) of its own becoming, and this processuality de-substantializes it. Spirit itself is thus radically de-substantialized: it is not a positive counter-force to nature, a different substance which gradually breaks and shines through the inert natural stuff; it is *nothing but* this process of freeing-itself-from. Hegel directly disowns the notion of Spirit as some kind of positive Agent which underlies the process:

> Spirit is usually spoken of as subject, as doing something, and apart from what it does, as this motion, this process, as still something particular, its activity being more or less contingent ... it is of the very nature of spirit to be this absolute liveliness, this process, to proceed forth from naturality, immediacy, to sublate, to quit its naturality, and to come to itself, and *to free itself*, it being itself only as it comes to itself as such a product of itself; *its actuality being merely that it has made itself into what it is*.[75]

The materialist reversal of Hegel in Ludwig Feuerbach and young Marx rejects this self-referential circularity, dismissing it as a case of idealist mystification: for Feuerbach and Marx, man is a *Gattungswesen* (being-of-genus) which asserts its life by way of realizing its 'essential forces'. The Hegelian event is thus undone; we are back at the Aristotelian ontology of substantial entities endowed with essential qualities.

STOP 5

The Three Events of Psychoanalysis

In his *Arcades Project*, Walter Benjamin[76] quotes the French historian André Monglond: 'The past has left images of itself in literary texts, images comparable to those which are imprinted by light on a photosensitive plate. The future alone possesses developers active enough to scan such surfaces perfectly.'[77] Far from being just a neutral observation about the complex interdependence of literary texts, this notion of past texts pointing towards the future is grounded in Benjamin's basic notion of the revolutionary act as the retroactive redemption of past failed acts:

> The past carries with it a temporal index by which it is referred to redemption. There is a secret agreement between past generations and the present one. Our coming was expected on earth. Like every generation that preceded us, we have been endowed with a weak Messianic power, a power to which the past has a claim.[78]

The first name that arises here is Shakespeare's, whose ability to prefigure insights which properly belong to later epochs often borders on the uncanny. Well before Satan's famous 'Evil, be thou my Good?' from Milton's *Paradise Lost*, the formula of the diabolical Evil was provided by Shakespeare, in whose *Titus Andronicus* the unrepentant Aaron's final words are: 'If one good deed in all my life I did, / I do repent it from my very soul.'[79] And Richard Wagner's short-circuit between seeing and hearing in the last act of *Tristan*, which is often perceived as the defining moment of modernism proper (the dying Tristan *sees* Isolde's voice) was clearly formulated already in *A Midsummer Night's Dream*. In Act V: 1, Bottom/Pyramus says: 'I see a voice: now will I to the chink, / To spy an I can hear my Thisbe's face.' (The same thought occurs later in *King Lear*: 'Look with thine ears.') And what about the extraordinarily modern definition of poetry, also from *A Midsummer Night's Dream*, Act V: 1, where Theseus says:

> The lunatic, the lover, and the poet,
> Are of imagination all compact:
> One sees more devils than vast hell can hold,
> That is, the madman; the lover, all as frantic,
> Sees Helen's beauty in a brow of Egypt:
> The poet's eye, in fine frenzy rolling,
> Doth glance from heaven to earth, from earth
>   to heaven;
> And, as imagination bodies forth
> The forms of things unknown, the poet's pen
> Turns them to shapes, and gives to airy nothing
> A local habitation and a name.
> Such tricks hath strong imagination,
> That if it would but apprehend some joy,

It comprehends some bringer of that joy;
Or in the night, imagining some fear,
How easy is a bush suppos'd a bear!

Indeed, as the nineteenth-century Symbolist poet Mallarmé put it, poetry talks about '*ce seul objet dont le Néant s'honore*' ('that exclusive object wherein Nothingness takes pride'). More precisely, Shakespeare articulates here a triad: a madman sees devils everywhere (he misperceives a bush as a bear); a lover sees sublime beauty in an ordinary face; a poet 'gives to airy nothing a local habitation and a name'. In all three cases we have a gap between ordinary reality and a transcendent ethereal dimension, but this gap is gradually reduced: the madman simply misperceives a real object as something else, not seeing it for what it is (a bush is perceived as a threatening bear); a lover maintains the reality of the beloved object, which is not cancelled, but merely 'transubstantiated' into the appearance of a sublime dimension (the beloved's ordinary face is perceived as it is, but it is *as such* elevated – I see beauty *in* it, as it is); with a poet, transcendence is reduced to zero, i.e., empirical reality is 'transubstantiated' – not into an expression/materialization of some higher reality, but into a materialization of *nothing*. A madman directly *sees* God, he mistakes a person for God (or the Devil); a lover sees God (divine beauty) *in* a person; a poet only sees a person against the background of Nothingness.[80]

Maybe we can use this Shakespearean triad of lunatic, lover and poet as a tool to propose a classification of events based on the Lacanian triad of Imaginary, Symbolic and Real: a lunatic dwells in the imaginary dimension, confusing reality and imagination; a lover identifies the beloved person with the absolute Thing in a symbolic short-circuit between signifier and signified which nonetheless maintains the gap that for ever separates them (the lover knows very well that, in reality, his/her beloved is an ordinary person with all his or her failures and weaknesses); a poet makes a phenomenon emerge against the background of the void of the Real.

For Lacan, the Imaginary, the Symbolic and the Real are the three fundamental dimensions in which a human being dwells. The Imaginary dimension is our direct lived experience of reality, but also of our dreams and nightmares – it is the domain of appearing, of how things appear to us. The Symbolic dimension is what Lacan calls the 'big Other,' the invisible order that structures our experience of reality, the complex network of rules and meanings which makes us see what we see the way we see it (and what we don't see the way we don't see it). The Real, however, is not simply external reality; it is rather, as Lacan put it, 'impossible': something which can neither be directly experienced nor symbolized – like a traumatic encounter of extreme violence which destabilizes our entire universe of meaning. As such, the Real can only be discerned in its traces, effects or aftershocks.

This triad is far from exclusively Lacanian – another version of it was proposed by Karl Popper (1902–94) in his theory of the Third World (which is Popper's name for the symbolic dimension or order).[81] Popper became aware that the usual classification of all phenomena into external material reality (from atoms to arms) and our inner psychic reality (of emotions, wishes, experiences) is not enough: ideas we talk about are not just passing thoughts in our minds, since these thoughts refer to something which remains the same while our thoughts pass away or change (when I think about 2+2=4 and my colleague thinks about it, we are thinking about the same thing, although our thoughts are materially different; when, in a conversation, a group of people talk about a triangle, they somehow talk about the same thing). Popper is, of course, not an Idealist: ideas do not exist independently of our minds, they are the result of our mental operations, but they are nonetheless not directly reducible to them – they possess a minimum of ideal objectivity. It is in order to capture this realm of ideal objects that Popper coined the term 'Third World,' and this Third World vaguely fits the Lacanian 'big Other'. However, the word 'order' should not lead us astray here: Lacan's symbolic order is not a fixed network of ideal categories or norms. The standard deconstructionist/feminist reproach to the Lacanian theory targets its alleged implicit normative content: Lacan's notion of the Name-of-the-Father, the agent of the symbolic Law which regulates sexual difference, allegedly introduces a norm which, even if it is never fully actualized, nonetheless imposes a standard on sexuality, somehow excluding those who occupy a marginal position (gays, transsexuals, etc.); furthermore, this norm is clearly historically conditioned, it is not a universal feature of being human, as Lacan allegedly claims. However, this reproach to Lacan relies on confusion apropos the word 'order' in the phrase 'symbolic order':

> 'Order,' in the legitimate sense of the term, designates nothing more than a specific domain: it does not

> indicate an order to be respected or obeyed, and even less an ideal to be conformed to or a harmony. The symbolic in Lacan's sense says nothing but the essential disorder which emerges at the juncture of language and the sexual.[82]

The Lacanian symbolic order is thus inherently inconsistent, antagonistic, flawed, 'barred,' an order of fictions whose authority is that of a fraud. It is on account of this inconsistency that, for Lacan, the three dimensions of Imaginary, Real and Symbolic are worlds intertwined like the famous Escher drawing 'Waterfall,' which shows a perpetually descending circuit of water. Our question here is: what type of event fits each of these dimensions? What is an imaginary event, a real event, a symbolic event? The question is so vast that we cannot deal with it in one stop – we have to change lines and make three connections from this stop.

Connection 5.1 – The Real: Confronting the Thing

The Japanese expression *bakku-shan* means 'a girl who looks as though she might be pretty when seen from behind, but isn't when seen from the front'. One of the lessons of the history of religion – and even more of today's experience of religion – is that the same holds for God himself: he may appear great when he is seen from behind and from a proper distance, but when he comes too close and we have to confront him face to face, spiritual bliss turns into horror. This destructive aspect of the divine, the brutal explosion of rage mixed with ecstatic bliss, is what Lacan aims at with his statement that gods belong to the Real. Such a traumatic encounter of a divine Thing is the Event as real.

The problem of Judaism is precisely: how are we to keep this dimension of the divine madness, of gods as real, at a distance? The Jewish god is also the god of brutal madness – what changes is the believers' stance towards this dimension of the divine: if we get too close to it, then 'the glory of the Lord is like devouring fire' (Exodus 24:17). This is why the Jewish people say to Moses: 'You speak to us, and we will listen. But don't let God speak directly to us, or we will die!' (Exodus 20:19) So what if, as Emmanuel Levinas[83] surmised, the ultimate addressee of the biblical commandment 'Don't kill' is God (Yahweh) himself, and we, fragile humans, are his neighbours exposed to divine rage? How often in the Old Testament do we encounter God as a dark stranger who brutally intrudes into human lives and sows destruction?

> On the way, at a place where Moses and his family spent the night, Yahweh met him and tried to kill him. But Zipporah took a flint, cut off her son's foreskin, and touched his feet with it, saying: 'This blood will protect you.' So Yahweh let Moses alone. Then she said, 'Protected by the blood of circumcision.' (Exodus 4:24–26)

Indeed, when Levinas wrote that the first reaction when we see a neighbour is to kill him, is the implication not that this primarily refers to God's relationship to humans, so that the commandment 'Don't kill' is an appeal to God to control his rage? Insofar as the Jewish solution is a dead god, a god who survives only as a 'dead letter' of the sacred book, of the Law to be interpreted, what dies with the death of God is precisely the god of the real, of destructive fury and revenge. The title of a well-known book on the Holocaust – *God Died in Auschwitz* – has thus to be turned around: God became alive in Auschwitz. There is a story from the Talmud about two rabbis debating a theological point. The one who is losing the debate calls upon God himself to come and decide, and when God effectively comes, the other rabbi tells him that his work of creation is already accomplished, so he has now nothing to say and should leave, which God does. It is as if, in Auschwitz, God comes back, with catastrophic consequences. The true horror does not occur when we are abandoned by God, but when God comes too close to us.

Recently this paradox was succinctly formulated by Jürgen Habermas: 'Secular languages which only eliminate the substance once intended leave irritations. When sin was converted to culpability, and the breaking of divine commands to an offence against human laws, something was lost.'[84] Which is why the secular-humanist reactions to phenomena like the Holocaust or Gulag are experienced as insufficient: in order to be at the level of such phenomena, something much stronger is needed, something akin to the old religious topic of a cosmic perversion or catastrophe in which the world itself is 'out of joint'. When one confronts a phenomenon like the Holocaust, the only appropriate reaction is the perplexed question 'Why did the heavens not darken?' (the title of Arno Mayor's famous book on the subject). Therein resides the paradox of the theological significance of holocaust: although it is usually conceived as the ultimate challenge to theology (if there is a God and if he is good, how could he have allowed such a horror to take place?), it is at the same time *only theology which can provide the frame enabling us to somehow approach the scope of this catastrophe* – the fiasco of God is still the fiasco of *God*.

Judaism provides a unique solution to this threat of the divine over-proximity: while, in pagan religions the gods were alive, Jewish believers already took God's death into account – and indications of this awareness abound in the Jewish sacred texts. Recall the story above about the two rabbis who basically tell God to shut up: they fight over a theological question until, unable to resolve it, one of them proposes: 'Let Heaven itself testify that the Law is according to my judgment.' A voice from heaven agrees with the rabbi who first appealed; however, the other rabbi then stands up and claims that even a voice from heaven was not to be regarded, 'For Thou, O God, didst long ago write down in the law which Thou gavest on Sinai, "Thou shalt follow the multitude."' God himself had to agree: after saying 'My children have vanquished me! My children have vanquished me!', he runs away. There is a similar story in the Babylonian Talmud (*Baba Metzia* 59b), but here, in a wonderful Nietzschean twist, God accepts his defeat with joyous laughter: Rabbi Nathan met the prophet Elijah and asked him, 'What did the Holy One do at that moment?' Elijah replied, 'He laughed [with joy], saying, "My children have defeated me, my children have defeated me."' The outstanding feature of this story is not only the divine laughter which replaces the sorrowful complaint, but the way the Sages (who stand for the big Other, the symbolic order, of course) win the argument against God: even God Himself, the absolute Subject, is decentred with regard to the big Other, so that, once his injunctions are written down, he can no longer touch them. We can thus imagine why God reacts to his defeat with joyous laughter: the Sages have learnt his lesson, that God is dead, and that the Truth resides in the dead letter of the Law which is beyond his control. In short, after the act of creation is accomplished, God loses even the right to intervene in how people interpret his law.

However, the living god continues his subterranean life and erratically returns in multiple forms, which are all guises of the monstrous Thing – up to today's popular culture. Nima Nourizadeh's 2012 film *Project X* narrates the birth of an urban legend: Thomas is turning seventeen, and his friends Costa and JB are planning to throw a huge birthday bash at Thomas's house to increase their popularity among their schoolmates. As Thomas's parents are going away for the weekend, Thomas's father lays down the rules (a maximum of five people at their house, not to drive his expensive Mercedes, and no one is allowed in his office).

Thomas worries that no one will come until, suddenly, cars start pulling up in the neighbourhood and the party becomes an instant hit. Gradually, things get out of control: the noise and scope of the party causes televised news coverage; news helicopters fly over the house; the police arrive with a SWAT team, which decides to let the party burn itself out before moving in. But then an intruder with a flamethrower torches trees around the neighbourhood and cars parked on the road, and the neighbourhood is left in flames until fire department helicopters extinguish it. When, the next morning, his parents do come home, Thomas's father punishes him by using his college funds to pay for the damage; but he nonetheless commends Thomas for the party – Thomas has shown he has guts, while his father thought he was a coward and a loser. The father's recognition demonstrates how the paternal prohibition functions:

> In fact, the image of the ideal Father is a neurotic's fantasy. Beyond the Mother … stands out the image of a father who would turn a blind eye to desires. This marks – more than it reveals – the true function of the Father, which is fundamentally to unite (and not to oppose) a desire to the Law.[85]

While prohibiting his son's escapades, the father not only discreetly ignores and tolerates them, but even solicits them. It is in this sense that Father as the agent of prohibition/law sustains desire/pleasures: there is no direct access to enjoyment since its very space is opened up by the blanks of the Father's controlling gaze. (And does exactly the same not hold for God himself, our ultimate father? The first commandment says: 'You shall have no other gods before me.' What does the ambiguous 'before me' refer to? Most translators agree that it means 'before my face, in front of me, when I see you' – which subtly implies that the jealous God will nonetheless turn a blind eye to what we are doing secretly, out of (his) sight. In short, God is like a jealous husband who tells his wife: 'OK, you can have other men, but do it discreetly, so that I (or the public in general) will not notice it and you will not put me to shame!') The negative proof of this constitutive role of the Father in carving out the space for viable enjoyment is the deadlock of today's permissiveness, where the master/expert no longer prohibits enjoyment but enjoins it ('sex is healthy,' etc.), thereby effectively sabotaging it.

How, then, does the figure of the father relate to the Thing? The father's symbolic authority functions as the agency which normalizes the encounter of the Thing: on behalf of the Law which regulates social interaction, the father signals his tolerance for occasional encounters of the Thing. But more relevant is the quasi-sacred character of the party: when it runs out of control, it explodes into what one cannot but designate as a collective experience of the sacred, an experience of what Georges Bataille[86] called *économie générale*, unrestrained expenditure, something like the dance of the Bacchantes reinvented for today, a moment when the lowest stupid adolescent partying turns into its opposite, a new form of the Sacred. And, to avoid a misunderstanding, the point is not to celebrate wild partying but to render visible the amphibious nature of the sacred itself. Russian filmmaker Sergei Eisenstein saw the production of pathos as a structural issue, not only as a matter of content. In *The General Line* (aka *The Old and the New*), there is a famous scene which renders the successful testing of a collective farm's new milk separator, with the enraptured farmers watching how the white liquid starts to flow out – the machine becomes a grail-like magic object which 'intensifies' their emotions.[87] Is it not exactly the same in *Project X* where a vulgar adolescent party is 'intensified' to a sacred orgy?

An even more extreme case of such 'intensification' is the pop-music event of the summer of 2012: 'Gangnam Style' performed by Psy, a South Korean singer. The song was not only wildly popular, it also mobilized people into a collective trance, with tens of thousands shouting and performing a dance that imitated horse riding, all in the same rhythm with an intensity unseen from the times of the early Beatles, referring to Psy as a new Messiah. The music is psydance at its worst, totally flat and mechanically simple, mostly computer-generated (the singer's name is, of course, a shortened version of 'psytrance'); what makes it interesting is the way it combines collective trance with self-irony. The words of the song (and the staging of the video clip) obviously poke fun at the meaninglessness and vacuity of Gangnam style (named after a trendy district of Seoul), some claim even in a subtly subversive way – but we are nonetheless entranced, caught up in the stupid marching rhythm, participating in it in pure mimesis; flash mobs popped up all around the world imitating the moments of the video. As a curiosity, it is worth noting that the 'Gangnam Style' video views surpassed even those of Justin Bieber's 'Baby' on YouTube, thus becoming the most watched YouTube video of all time. On 21 December 2012, it reached the magic number of one billion views – and since December 21 was the day when those who took seriously the predictions of the Mayan calendar were expecting the end of the world, one could say that the Ancient Mayans were right: the fact is that the 'Gangnam Style' video effectively *is* the sign of the collapse of civilization …

'Gangnam Style' is not ideology in spite of ironic distance, it is ideology because of it: irony plays the same role as the documentary style in Lars von Trier's *Breaking the Waves*, in which the subdued pseudo-documentary form makes palpable the excessive content – in a strictly homologous way, the self-mocking irony of 'Gangnam Style' makes palpable the stupid enjoyment of the rave music. Many listeners find the song disgustingly attractive, i.e., they 'love to hate it,' or, rather, they enjoy the very fact of finding it disgusting so they repeatedly play it to prolong their disgust. Such an ecstatic surrender to obscene *jouissance* in all its stupidity entangles the subject into what Lacan, following Freud, calls drive; perhaps its paradigmatic expressions are the repulsive private rituals (sniffing one's own sweat, sticking one's finger into one's nose, etc.) that bring intense satisfaction without our being aware of it – or, insofar as we are aware of it, without our being able to do anything to prevent it. In Hans Christian Andersen's fairy tale *The Red Shoes*, an impoverished young woman puts on a pair of magical shoes and almost dies when her feet won't stop dancing. She is only saved when an executioner cuts off her feet with his axe. Her still-shod feet dance on, whereas she is given wooden feet and finds peace in religion. These shoes stand for drive at its purest: an 'undead' partial object that functions as a kind of impersonal willing – 'it wants,' it persists in its repetitive movement (of dancing), it follows its path and exacts its satisfaction at any price, irrespective of the subject's well-being. This drive is that which is 'in the subject more than itself': although the subject cannot ever subjectivize it, assume it as its own by way of saying 'It is I who want to do this,' it nonetheless operates in its very kernel.

Lacan's thesis is that it is possible to sublimate this dangerous frenzy; this is what, ultimately, art and religion are about. Music turns into a sign of love when it no longer haunts the subject as the obscene *jouissance*, compelling it to surrender blindly to its disgusting rhythm, but when love transpires through its sounds – love as the acceptance of the Other in its radical otherness, a love which is, as Lacan put it in the very last page of his *Seminar XI*, beyond Law. But one should be very precise here: love beyond Law does not mean wild love outside all symbolic institutional co-ordinates (like Carmen's 'Love is a rebellious bird'); it means almost the exact opposite. The discerning feature of this love is indifference, not towards its object but towards the positive properties of the beloved object: to say 'I love you because you have a nice nose/attractive legs,' etc., is *a priori* false. With love it is the same as with religious belief: I do not love you because I find your positive features attractive, but, on the contrary, I find your positive features attractive because I love you and therefore observe you with a loving gaze.

• • •

The 2012 Nobel Prize for Economics went to Alvin Roth and Lloyd Shapley for their elaboration of 'matching theory,' the economics of choice when you aren't the only one choosing. In an interview, Roth explained: 'When [people] get into schools, when they choose careers, when they get married, these are all matching markets. You can't just choose what you want, you also have to be chosen. The utility of matching is that you are defining a relationship.' The key phrase here is 'defining a relationship': in matters of love, matching theory endeavours to construct a kind of axiom or formula of a successful sexual relationship. But can a love relationship be put on the same level as bringing together a kidney patient with a donor, or a job-seeker with a manager ready to hire? The problem is not the one of moral dignity, but of the immanent logic: when you fall in love, you don't just know what you need/want and look for the one who has it – the 'miracle' of love is that you learn what you need only when you find it.

How does all this relate to event in sexuality? In French filmmaker Catherine Breillat's *Romance* (1999), there is a fantasmatic scene which perfectly stages this radical split between love and sexuality: the heroine imagines herself lying naked on her belly on a low small table divided in the middle by a partition with a hole just big enough for her body. With the upper side of her body, she faces a nice tender guy with whom she exchanges gentle loving words and kisses, while her lower part is exposed to one or more sex-machine studs who penetrate her wildly and repeatedly. However, the true miracle occurs when these two series momentarily *coincide*, when sex is 'transubstantiated' into an act of love. There are four ways to disavow this impossible/real conjunction of love and sexual enjoyment: (1) the celebration of asexual 'pure' love, as if the sexual desire for the beloved demonstrates the love's inauthenticity; (2) the opposite assertion of intense sex as 'the only real thing,' which reduces love to a mere imaginary lure; (3) the division of these two aspects, their allocation to two different persons – one loves one's gentle wife (or the idealized inaccessible Lady), while one has sex with a 'vulgar' mistress; (4) or their false immediate merger, in which intense sex is supposed to demonstrate that one 'truly loves' one's partner, as if, in order to prove that our love is a true one, every sexual act has to be the proverbial 'fuck of the century'. All these four stances are wrong, an escape from assuming the impossible/real conjunction of love and sex; a true love is enough in itself, it makes sex irrelevant – but precisely because 'fundamentally, it doesn't matter,' we can fully enjoy it without any superego pressure. And, unexpectedly, this brings us to Lenin. When, in 1916, Lenin's (at that point ex-)mistress, Inessa Armand, wrote to him that even a fleeting passion was more poetic and cleaner than kisses without love between a man and woman, he replied:

> Kisses without love between vulgar spouses are *filthy*. I agree. These need to be contrasted ... with what? ... It would seem: kisses *with* love. But you contrast 'a fleeting (why a fleeting) passion (why not love?)' – and it comes out logically as if kisses without love (fleeting) are contrasted to marital kisses without love ... This is odd.[88]

Lenin's reply is usually dismissed as proof of his petit-bourgeois sexual constraint, sustained by his bitter memory of their past affair; however, there is more to it. The insight is that the marital 'kisses without love' and the extramarital 'fleeting affair' are two sides of the same coin – they both shirk from *combining* the Real of an unconditional passionate attachment with the form of symbolic proclamation. Lenin is deeply right here, although not in the standard prudish sense of preferring 'normal' marriage out of love to illicit promiscuity. The underlying insight is that, against all appearances, love and sex are not only distinct, but ultimately *incompatible*, that they operate at thoroughly different levels, like *agape* and *eros*: love is charitable, self-erasing, ashamed of itself, while sex is intense, self-assertive, possessing, inherently *violent* (or the opposite: possessive love versus generous indulging in sexual pleasures). However, the true miracle occurs when (exceptionally) these two series momentarily *coincide*, when sex is 'transubstantiated' into an act of love – an achievement which is real/impossible in the precise Lacanian sense, and as such marked by an inherent *rarity*. Today, it is as if the knot of three levels which characterized traditional sexuality (reproduction, sexual pleasure, love) is gradually dissolving: reproduction is left to biogenetic procedures which are making sexual intercourse redundant; sex itself is turned into recreational fun; while love is reduced to the domain of 'emotional fulfilment'. In such a situation, it is all the more precious to be reminded of those rare miraculous moments in which two of these three dimensions can still overlap, i.e., in which *jouissance* becomes a sign of love. It is only in these rare moments that sexual activity becomes an authentic Event.

Connection 5.2 – The Symbolic: The New Harmony

> A tap of your finger on the drum releases all sounds
> and initiates the new harmony.
> A step of yours is the conscription of the new men
> and their marching orders.
> You look away: the new love!
> You look back, — the new love!
> 'Change our fates, shoot down the plagues, beginning
> with time,' the children sing to you. 'Build wher-
> ever you can the substance of our fortunes and our
> wishes,' they beg you.
> Arriving from always, you'll go away everywhere.[89]

These lines from Arthur Rimbaud's '*À une raison*' ('To a Reason') provide the most succinct determination of the *symbolic event*, which is the emergence of a new Master-Signifier. This evental moment is the moment when the signifier – a physical form that represents meaning – falls into the signified, into what it means, when the signifier becomes part of the object it designates. Let us imagine a situation of social disarray in which different social groups have different expectations, projects and dreams; some agent then succeeds in bringing them together under the banner of a Master-Signifier which does not obliterate these differences by way of focusing on the common ground (the shared visions and values) of the groups – it merely allows each of the groups to recognize its own content in the shared signifier. Let us say this signifier is 'solidarity': it will mean a different thing to an unemployed worker, to a conservative farmer, to a starved intellectual, to a soldier or policeman, etc., etc.; however, the social pact, the unity, this signifier will impose will nonetheless not be simply illusory, i.e., it will not be just an imaginary mask covering up differences which continue to exist. Insofar as the imposition of this signifier serves as the focal point of for actual political movement which eventually even takes power, *it establishes its own social reality*: people effectively collaborate, even if it appears to them that they all do it for their own purpose. It doesn't matter if some groups use this signifier cynically – what matters is that they participate in the social-symbolic space under its banner. In this way, following Marx's analysis of the Party of Order which took power when the 1848 revolutionary élan in France dwindled, the secret of its existence was:

> the coalition of Orléanists and Legitimists into one party, disclosed. The bourgeois class fell apart into two big factions which alternately – the big landed proprietors under the restored monarchy and the finance aristocracy and the industrial bourgeoisie under the July Monarchy – had maintained a monopoly of power. Bourbon was the royal name for the predominant influence of the interests of the one faction, Orléans the royal name for the predominant influence of the interests of the other faction – the nameless realm of the republic was the only one in which both factions could maintain with equal power the common class interest without giving up their mutual rivalry.[90]

The parliamentary députés of the Party of Order perceived their republicanism as a charade: in parliamentary debates, they generated royalist slips of tongue and ridiculed the Republic to let it be known that their true aim was to restore the monarchy. What they were not aware of is that they themselves were duped as to the true social impact of their rule. They unknowingly established the conditions of bourgeois republican order that they despised so much (by, for instance, guaranteeing the safety of private property). So it is not that they were royalists who were just wearing republican masks, although they experienced themselves as such; it was their 'inner' royalist conviction which was the deceptive front masking their true social role. In short, far from being the hidden truth of their public republicanism, their sincere royalism was the fantasmatic support of their actual republicanism – it was what provided the passion to their activity. Is it not, then, that the députés of the Party of Order were also *feigning to feign* to be republicans, to be what they really were?

Such a signifying reversal (the imposition of a Master-Signifier) is not simply external to the designated thing: what it does to the thing is to provide it with an additional unknowable feature which appears as the hidden origin of its properties. Imagine the name of one's nation as the Master-Signifier: if we ask a member of that nation, 'What does it mean to be American/Russian/British?' the answer will never be just a series of observable properties, but always something like: 'It is something mysterious which makes us American/Russian/British and accounts for all observable features; it's something that foreigners cannot understand – to feel it you have to be one of us!' The fact that this mysterious X appears deeper than language, beyond clear linguistic articulation, is an effect of the very excess of language over its object.

A speech act thus becomes a symbolic Event if and when its occurrence restructures the entire field: although there is no new content, everything is somehow thoroughly different. Gilles Deleuze elaborated this dimension in his notion of a *pure past*: not the past into which present things pass, but an absolute past 'where all events, including those that have sunk without trace, are stored and remembered as their passing away'[91]; a virtual past which already contains things which are still present. The present can become the past because in a way it is already – it can perceive itself as part of the past ('what we are doing now is (will have been) history'): 'It is with respect to the pure element of the past, understood as the past in general, as an *a priori* past, that a given former present is reproducible and the present present is able to reflect itself.'[92] Does this mean that this pure past involves a thoroughly deterministic notion of the universe in which everything to happen (to come), all actual spatial-temporal deployment, is already part of an immemorial/atemporal virtual network? No, and for a very precise reason: because 'the pure past must be all the past but must also be amenable to change through the occurrence of any new present'.[93] It was that great conservative T. S. Eliot who first clearly formulated this link between our dependence on tradition and our power to change the past:

> the historical sense involves a perception, not only of the pastness of the past, but of its presence; the

historical sense compels a man to write not merely with his own generation in his bones, but with a feeling that the whole of the literature of Europe from Homer and within it the whole of the literature of his own country has a simultaneous existence and composes a simultaneous order … No poet, no artist of any art, has his complete meaning alone. His significance, his appreciation is the appreciation of his relation to the dead poets and artists. You cannot value him alone; you must set him, for contrast and comparison, among the dead … The necessity that he shall conform, that he shall cohere, is not one-sided; what happens when a new work of art is created is something that happens simultaneously to all the works of art which preceded it. The existing monuments form an ideal order among themselves, which is modified by the introduction of the new (the really new) work of art among them. The existing order is complete before the new work arrives; for order to persist after the supervention of novelty, the *whole* existing order must be, if ever so slightly, altered; and so the relations, proportions, values of each work of art toward the whole are readjusted; and this is conformity between the old and the new … the past should be altered by the present as much as the present is directed by the past. And the poet who is aware of this will be aware of great difficulties and responsibilities.[94]

When Eliot writes that, when judging a living poet, 'you must set him … among the dead,' he formulates precisely an example of Deleuze's pure past. And when he writes that 'the existing order is complete before the new work arrives; for order to persist after the supervention of novelty, the *whole* existing order must be, if ever so slightly, altered; and so the relations, proportions, values of each work of art toward the whole are readjusted,' he no less clearly formulates the paradoxical link between the completeness of the past and our capacity to change it retroactively: precisely because the pure past is complete, each new work rearranges its entire balance. Take Argentine writer Jorge Luis Borges' precise formulation of the relationship between Kafka and the multitude of his precursors, from old Chinese authors to Robert Browning: 'Kafka's idiosyncrasy, in greater or lesser degree, is present in each of these writings, but if Kafka had not written we would not perceive it; that is to say, it would not exist ... each writer *creates* his precursors. His work modifies our conception of the past, as it will modify the future.'[95] The properly dialectical solution of the dilemma of 'Is it really there, in the source, or did we only read it into the source?' is thus: it is there, but we can only perceive and state this retroactively, from today's perspective.

Here, the contemporary Canadian philosopher Peter Hallward falls short in his otherwise excellent *Out of This World*[96] where he stresses only the aspect of the pure past as the virtual field in which the fate of all actual events is sealed in advance, since 'everything is already written' in it: he ignores the retroactive movement on which Deleuze also insists, i.e., how is this eternal pure past which fully determines us itself subjected to retroactive change? What resonates in this topic is, of course, the Protestant belief of predestination: far from being a reactionary theological motif, predestination is a key element of the materialist theory of sense. Predestination does not mean that our fate is sealed in an actual text that has existed from eternity in the divine mind; the text which predestines us belongs to the purely virtual eternal past which, as such, can be retroactively rewritten by our acts. This, perhaps, is the ultimate meaning of the singularity of Christ's incarnation: it is an *act* which radically changes our destiny. Prior to Christ, we were determined by Fate, caught in the cycle of sin and its payment, while Christ's erasing of our past sins means precisely that his sacrifice changes our virtual past and thus sets us free. When Deleuze writes that 'my wound existed before me; I was born to embody it,'[97] does this variation on the Cheshire cat and its smile from *Alice in Wonderland* (the cat was born to embody its smile) not provide a perfect formula of Christ's sacrifice: Christ was born to embody his wound, to be crucified? The problem is the literal teleological reading of this proposition, as if the actual deeds of a person merely actualize his or her atemporal-eternal fate inscribed in their virtual idea:

> Caesar's only real task is to become worthy of the events he has been created to embody. *Amor fati.* What Caesar actually does adds nothing to what he virtually is. When Caesar actually crosses the Rubicon this involves no deliberation or choice since it is simply part of the entire, immediate expression of Caesarness, it simply unrolls or 'unfolds' something that was encompassed for all times in the notion of Caesar.[98]

However, what about the retroactivity of a gesture which

(re)constitutes this past itself? This, perhaps, is the most succinct definition of what an authentic act is: in our ordinary activity, we effectively just follow the (virtual-fantasmatic) co-ordinates of our identity, while an act proper is the paradox of an actual move which (retroactively) changes the very virtual, 'transcendental' co-ordinates of its agent's being – or, in Freudian terms, which does not only change the actuality of our world, but also 'moves its underground'. We have thus a kind of reflexive 'folding back of the condition onto the given it was the condition for'[99]: while the pure past is the transcendental condition for our acts, our acts do not only create new actual reality, they also retroactively change this very condition. This is how one should also read Hegel's thesis that, in the course of the dialectical development things 'become what they are': it is not that a temporal deployment merely actualizes some pre-existing atemporal conceptual structure – this atemporal conceptual structure itself is the result of contingent temporal decisions. Let us take the exemplary case of a contingent decision whose outcome defines the agent's entire life: Caesar's crossing of the Rubicon:

> It is not enough to say that crossing Rubicon is part of the complete notion of Caesar. One should rather say that Caesar is defined by the fact that he crossed Rubicon. His life didn't follow a scenario written in the book of some goddess: there is no book which would already have contained the relations of Caesar's life, for the simple reason that his life itself is this book, and that, at every moment, an event is in itself its own narrative.[100]

Does exactly the same not hold for love? Falling in love is a contingent encounter, but once it occurs, it appears as necessary, as something towards which my entire life was moving. Lacan described this reversal of contingency into necessity as a shift from the 'stops not being written' to the 'doesn't stop being written': first, love 'stops not being written,' it emerges through a contingent encounter; then, once it is here, it 'doesn't stop being written,' it imposes on a lover the work of love, the continuous effort to inscribe into his/her being all the consequences of love, to structure his/her love around the fidelity to the event of love:

> The displacement of the negation from the 'stops not being written' to the 'doesn't stop being written,' in other words, from contingency to necessity – there lies the point of suspension to which all love is attached. All love, subsisting only on the basis of the 'stops not being written,' tends to make the negation shift to the 'doesn't stop being written,' doesn't stop, won't stop.[101]

Therein resides the dialectical reversal of contingency into necessity, i.e., the way the outcome of a contingent process is the appearance of necessity: things retroactively 'will have been' necessary, or, to quote Jean-Pierre Dupuy: 'It is thus the event's actualization – the fact that it takes place – which retroactively creates its necessity.'[102] Dupuy provides the example of the French presidential elections in May 1995; here is the January forecast of the main French polling institute: 'If, on next May 8, M Balladur will be elected, one can say that the presidential election was decided before it even took place.'

If – accidentally – an event takes place, it creates the preceding chain which makes it appear inevitable.

This brings us to the specific temporality of the symbolic event: the abrupt reversal of 'not yet' into 'always-already'. There is always a gap between formal and material change: things gradually change at the material level, and this change is subterranean, like a secret spreading of a deadly infection; when the struggle erupts into the open, the mole has already finished its work and the battle is *de facto* over – all one has to do is to remind those in power to look down and perceive how there is no longer any ground under their feet, and the whole edifice collapses like a house of cards. When Margaret Thatcher was asked what her greatest achievement was, she answered: 'New Labour.' And she was right: her triumph was that even her political enemies adopted her basic economic policies – the true triumph is not the victory over the enemy, it occurs when the enemy itself starts to use your language, so that your ideas form the foundation of the entire field. The same holds for the great polemics between John Locke and Robert Filmer in the seventeenth century: Filmer opposed Locke and the Enlightenment notion that all men are created equal in the state of nature by God, and that as such they possess a series of natural rights, claiming instead that the government of a family by the father is the true origin and model of all government. In the beginning God gave authority to Adam; from Adam this authority was inherited by Noah, etc., so that the patriarchs inherited the absolute power which they exercised over their families and servants; and it is from these patriarchs that all kings and governors derive their authority, which is therefore absolute and founded upon divine right. The problem is that, in engaging in this kind of rational disputation, Filmer already moves on to the terrain determined by his opponent, the terrain of the natural history of society. Here is, at a more universal level, Hegel's classic description of how the pure insight of the Enlightenment undermines traditional religious spirit:

> The communication of pure insight is on that account comparable to a silent extension or the expansion, say, of a scent in the unresisting atmosphere. It is a penetrating infection, which did not previously make itself noticeable as something distinct from and opposed to the indifferent medium into which it insinuates its way, and hence cannot be averted. Only when the infection has become widespread is that consciousness alive to it, which unconcernedly yielded to its influence ... In the condition, therefore, in which consciousness becomes aware of pure insight, this insight is already widespread. The struggle with it betrays the fact that the infection has done its work. The struggle is too late; and every means taken merely makes the disease worse; for the disease has seized the very marrow of spiritual life ... being now an invisible and unperceived spirit, it insinuates its way through and through the noble parts, and soon has got complete hold over all the vitals and members of the unconscious idol; and then 'some fine morning it gives its comrade a shove with the elbow, when, bash! crash! – and the idol is lying on the floor'.[103]

We all know the classic scene in cartoons: the cat reaches a precipice but goes on walking, ignoring the fact that there is no ground under its feet; it starts to fall only when it looks down and notices the abyss. When a political regime, say, loses its authority, it is like that cat above the precipice: in order to fall, it only has to be reminded to look down. But the opposite also holds: when an authoritarian regime approaches its final crisis, its dissolution as a rule follows two steps. Before its actual collapse, a mysterious rupture takes place: all of a sudden people know that the game is over – they are simply no longer afraid. It is not only that the regime loses its legitimacy, its exercise of power itself is perceived as an impotent panic reaction. In *Shah of Shahs*, a classic account of the Iranian revolution of 1979, Ryszard Kapuściński located the precise moment of this rupture: at a Tehran crossroad, a single demonstrator refused to budge when a policeman shouted at him to move, and the embarrassed policeman simply withdrew; in a couple of hours, all Tehran knew about this incident, and although there were street fights going on for weeks, everyone somehow knew the game was over.[104]

This brings us back to (falling in) love, which is characterized by the same temporal gap. In one of Henry James's stories, the hero says about a woman close to him: 'She already loves him, she just doesn't know it yet.' What we find here is a kind of Freudian counterpart of Benjamin Libet's famous experiment about free will: Libet demonstrated that, even before we consciously decide (say, to move a finger), the appropriate neuronal processes are already underway, which means that our conscious decision just takes note of what is already going on (adding its superfluous authorization to a *fait accompli*).[105]

With Freud, decision is also prior to consciousness – however, it is not a purely objective process but an unconscious decision. Freud here is in agreement with Schelling for whom also a truly free decision is unconscious, which is why we never fall in love in present time: after a (usually long) process of subconscious gestation, we all of a sudden become aware that we (already) *are* in love. The Fall (into love) never *happens* at a certain moment, it has *always-already happened*.

With regard to the general economy of Wagner's work, the long narratives which interrupt the flow of events (especially in his late operas), where the singer recapitulates what went on before the opera or, often, simply in the previous act, cannot but appear as a symptom of the inherent failure of the entire body of work: instead of the organic direct rendering of events – we get their artificial narrative representation.[106] What, however, if these narrative passages obey a very precise performative logic of the 'declarative'? One does something; one counts oneself as (declares oneself) the one who did it; and, on the basis of this declaration, one does something new – the proper moment of subjective transformation occurs at the moment of declaration, not at the moment of the act. In other words, the truly New emerges through narrative, the apparently purely reproductive retelling of what happened – it is this retelling that opens up the space (the possibility) of acting in a new way. Furious about his treatment, a worker participates in a wildcat strike, say; however, it is only when, in the aftermath of his action, he counts/retells it as an act of class struggle that the worker subjectively transforms himself into the revolutionary subject, and, on the basis of this transformation, he can go on acting as a true revolutionary. Nowhere is this 'performative' role of retelling more palpable than in what philistines consider the most boring passages of Wagner's musical dramas, the long narratives in which the hero recapitulates what went on until that point. As Alain Badiou pointed out,[107] these long narratives are the true sites of dramatic shift – in the course of them, we witness the narrator's profound subjective transformation. Exemplary here is Wotan's great monologue in Act II of *Die Walküre*: the Wotan who emerges as the result of his own narrative is not the same Wotan as the one who embarked upon it, but a Wotan who decided to act in a new way – Wotan sees and accepts his ultimate failure, and decides to desire his own end. And, as Badiou noted, it is the role of the musical texture which is crucial here: it is the music which changes (what may sound like) a report on the events and state of the world into the deployment of the subjective metamorphosis of the narrator himself. One can also see how right Wagner was to reduce the actual act (a battle, usually) to an insignificant occurrence to be disposed off quickly, preferably even off stage (as is the case, at the beginning of Act II of *Parsifal*, with Parsifal's fight with and victory over Klingsor's knights: it takes place off stage, we only hear the report on Parsifal's progress by Klingsor who observes the fight from afar): it is impossible not to note how strangely the brevity of actual fights in Wagner's works (the brief duel between Lohengrin and Telramund in Act III of *Lohengrin*; the duel between Tristan and Melot at the end of Act III of *Tristan*, not to mention the ridiculous fights at the end of *Tristan*) contrasts with the long duration of narratives and declarations.

The same temporality characterizes structuralism – no wonder Claude Lévi-Strauss (1908–2009) designated structuralism as transcendentalism without a transcendental subject. In a unique case of self-reference, the ultimate case of a symbolic event, of something emerging all of a sudden and creating its own past, is the emergence of the symbolic order itself. The structuralist idea is that one cannot think the genesis of the symbolic (order): once it is here, this order is *always-already* here, one cannot step outside it; all one can do is to tell myths about its genesis (which Lacan engages in occasionally). Inverting the wonderful title of Alexei Yurchak's book about the last Soviet generation – *Everything Was Forever, Until It Was No More* – nothing of the symbolic order was here, until all of it was all of a sudden *always-already* here. The problem here is the emergence of a self-relating 'closed' system which has no outside: it cannot be explained from outside because its constitutive act is self-relating, i.e., the system fully emerges once it starts to cause itself; it posits its presuppositions in a closed loop. So it's not just that the symbolic order is all of a sudden fully here – there was nothing, and a moment later it is all here – but there is nothing and then, all of a sudden, it is as if the symbolic order was always-already here, as if there was never a time without it.

Connection 5.3 – The Imaginary: The Three Splashes

There are pieces of classical music which, in our culture, became so deeply associated with their later use in some product of commercial popular culture that it is almost impossible to dissociate them from this use. Since the theme of the second movement of Mozart's Piano Concerto No. 20 was used in *Elvira Madigan*, a popular Swedish melodrama, this piece is even now regularly characterized as the 'Elvira Madigan' concerto even by serious classical music labels. But what if, instead of exploding in rage against such commercialized music fetishism, one makes an exception and openly confesses the guilty pleasure of enjoying a piece of music which is in itself worthless and draws all its interest from the way it has been used in a product of popular culture? My favourite candidate is the 'Storm Clouds Cantata' from the Hitchcock film *The Man Who Knew Too Much*, composed by Arthur Benjamin especially for the climactic scene at the Royal Albert Hall. Although the Cantata is a rather ridiculous piece of late-Romantic kitsch, it is not as devoid of interest as one may think – already the words (by D. B. Wyndham-Lewis) are worth quoting:

There came a whispered terror on the breeze
And the dark forest shook
And on the trembling trees
Came the nameless fear
And panic overtook each flying creature of the wild
And when they all had fled
Yet stood the trees
Around whose heads
Screaming
The night birds wheeled and shot away
Finding release
From that which drove them onward like their prey
The storm clouds broke and drowned the dying moon

The storm clouds broke
Finding release

Is this not a minimal scenario of what Gilles Deleuze called an 'abstract' emotion-event: a peace full of tension, which grows unbearable and is finally released in a violent explosion? One should recall here Hitchcock's dream of bypassing the narrative audio-visual medium altogether and provoking emotions in the spectator directly, manipulating through a complex mechanism his emotional neuronal centres. To put it in Platonic terms: *Psycho* is really not a film about pathological or terrorized persons, but about the 'abstract' Idea of Terror which is represented in concrete individuals and their misfortunes. In the same way, the music of the 'Storm Clouds Cantata' does not illustrate Wyndham-Lewis's words, and even less does it refer to the cinema narrative. On the contrary; it directly renders the emotion-event.

Such an event is imaginary in the strict Lacanian sense: it floats at a distance from its material support which represents and generates it, in the fragile surface domain between being and non-being. In his *Logic of Sense*, Gilles Deleuze inverts Plato's dualism of eternal Ideas and their imitations in sensuous reality into the dualism of substantial (material) bodies and the pure impassive surface of Sense, the flux of Becoming which is to be located on the very borderline of Being and non-Being. Senses are surfaces which do not exist, but merely subsist: 'They are not things or facts, but events. We cannot say that they exist, but rather that they subsist or inhere (having this minimum of being which is appropriate to that which is not a thing, a nonexisting entity.'[108] The ancient Stoics, who developed this notion of 'incorporeals,' were

> the first to reverse Platonism and to bring about a radical inversion. For if bodies with their states, qualities, and quantities, assume all the characteristics of substance and cause, conversely, the characteristics of the Idea are relegated to the other side, that is to this impassive extra-Being which is sterile, inefficacious, and on the surface of things: the ideational or the incorporeal can no longer be anything other than an 'effect'.[109]

The knife and the flesh are bodies; the knife is the cause of an asomatic *kategorema* (predicate), namely being cut, with respect to the flesh. Fire and wood are bodies; the fire is the cause of an asomatic *kategorema*, namely being burnt, with respect to the wood. If the sun or the sun's heat makes the wax melt, we have to say that the sun is the cause, not of the melting of the wax, but of the wax being melted, of a *kategorema* which is indicated by an infinitive.

Buddhist ontology seems to point in a similar direction, even radicalizing it: reality itself is de-substantialized, reduced to a flow of fragile appearances, so that ultimately everything is event(al). The Buddhist universe thus allows for two types of events: the event of Enlightenment, of fully assuming the non-existence of the Self, and the unique capture of a fleeting event, exemplarily in haiku poetry and what Deleuze calls a pure event of (non)sense. This seems to be the infinite judgement of Buddhism: the overlapping of the Absolute (the primordial Void experienced in Nirvana) and the fragile flash-like tiny surface effect (the topic of haiku). Here is Matsuo Basho's best known haiku:

Old pond …
A frog jumps in
Splash

The true object is the splash-event (overlapping with the silence that sustains it?). There is no idealization in haiku, just the effect of sublimation where no matter how 'low' a material act can give birth to the event, so we should not be afraid to imagine a much more vulgar version of a haiku focused on the same event – a friend from Japan informed me that there is a twentieth-century variation on Basho's splash-motif which, precisely, should *not* be read as a parody:

Toilet bowl with stale water …
I sit on it
Splash

The three-lines-rule of a haiku poem is well-justified: the first line renders the pre-evental situation (a calm old pond, a bowl with calm water); the second line marks a cut into this inactivity, the intervention which disturbs peace and will generate the event (a frog jumps, I sit on a toilet bowl); and the last line names the fleeting event itself (the sound of splash). Even when the cutting word or phrase (*kireji*) is not followed by an active intervention, it marks a break between the general neutral situation and the particular element which serves as the material support of the event – here are two further haikus from Basho:

> Spring:
> A hill without a name
> Veiled in morning mist.
>
> The beginning of autumn:
> Sea and emerald paddy
> Both the same green.

The 'object' is here first the morning mist, then the colour green – object not as a substance but as an event, as a pure sterile effect in excess of its cause (which, as we have seen, can just as easily be vulgar as sublime). In such an immaterial effect, the fleeting almost-nothing of the pure appearance overlaps with eternity, movement overlaps with stillness, noise with eternal silence, a singular moment of sense with Non-Sense; it is the Zen way to say 'Spirit is a bone'. However, such a suspension of corporeal reality is profoundly ambiguous: it can also function as a screen obfuscating the horrifying consequences of our acts. Recall the title of Robert Pirsig's perennial bestseller of New Age philosophy, *Zen and the Art of Motorcycle Maintenance*[110]; one can easily imagine a series of variations on the same motif: Zen and the art of sexual performance, or business success ... up to Zen and the art of gentle warfare. Indeed, within the Zen attitude, the warrior no longer acts as a person; he is thoroughly de-subjectivized, or, as one of the main contributors to Zen's spread to the West, D. T. Suzuki, himself put it: 'it is really not he but the sword itself that does the killing. He had no desire to do harm to anybody, but the enemy appears and makes himself a victim. It is as though the sword performs automatically its function of justice, which is the function of mercy.'[111] Does this description of killing not provide the ultimate case of the phenomenological attitude which, instead of intervening into reality, just lets things appear as they are? The sword itself does the killing; the enemy just appears and makes himself a victim – the warrior is in it for nothing, reduced to the passive observer of his own acts.

In the 1970s, at the time of the military dictatorship in Brazil, the circle of secret policemen engaged in torturing political prisoners improvised a kind of private religion: a New Age Buddhist mixture based on the conviction that there is no reality, just a fragmented dance of illusory appearances.[112] One can well see how this 'religion' enabled them to endure the horror of what they were doing. No wonder, then, that, 'struck by his leader's cold demeanour and his utter ruthlessness towards their enemies, one of his comrades once compared Pol Pot with a Buddhist monk who had attained the "third level" of consciousness: "You are completely neutral. Nothing moves you. This is the highest level."'[113] One should not dismiss this idea as an obscene false parallel: Pol Pot came from the Buddhist cultural background with its long tradition of militarist discipline. Along these lines, we can well invent yet another haiku whose third line renders the pure event of blood splashing from a body cut by sword:

Fat body wiggling in front of me
The swing of my sword
Splash!

Or, why not, a step further, in the direction of Auschwitz:

Prisoners take a shower
My finger presses a button
Cries echo!

The point of these improvisations is not to engage in tasteless jokes, but to make us see that a truly enlightened person should be able to see a pure event even in such terrifying circumstances. The sad lesson here is that there is no incompatibility between brutal terror and authentic poetic spirit – they can go together.

STOP 6

The Undoing of an Event

The German expression *rückgängig machen*, usually translated as to 'annul, cancel or unhitch,' has a more precise connotation: to retroactively undo something, to make it as if it didn't take place. The comparison between Mozart's *Marriage of Figaro* and Rossini's *Figaro*-esque operas makes this immediately clear. In Mozart, the emancipatory political potential of Beaumarchais's play survives the pressure of censorship – think only of the finale, where the Count has to kneel down and ask for forgiveness of his subjects (not to mention the explosion of the collective 'Viva la libertà!' in the finale of Act I of *Don Giovanni*). The breathtaking achievement of Rossini's *Barber of Seville* should be measured by this standard: Rossini took a theatrical piece which was one of the symbols of the French bourgeois revolutionary spirit, and totally de-politicized it, changing it into pure *opera buffa*. No wonder the golden years of Rossini were 1815 to 1830 – the years of reaction, the years in which the European powers tackled the impossible task of the *Ungeschehenmachen*, the undoing, the making-it-not-happen of the previous revolutionary decades. This is what Rossini did in his great comic operas: they try to bring back to life the innocence of the pre-revolutionary world. Rossini did not actively hate and fight the new world – he simply composed as if the years 1789–1815 didn't exist. Rossini was therefore right to (almost) stop composing after 1830 and to adopt the satisfied stance of a *bon vivant* making his tournedos. This was the only properly ethical thing to do, and his long silence is comparable to that of Jean Sibelius.

Insofar as the French Revolution is *the* Event of modern history, the break after which 'nothing was the same,' one should raise here the question: is this kind of 'undoing,' of dis-eventalization, one of the possible destinies of every Event? The well-known formula '*Je sais bien, mais quand même* …' ('I know very well, but nonetheless …') signals a divided stance of the subject towards an entity – one knows it is true, but one cannot really accept this truth, for example: 'I know very well my son is a murderer, but I nonetheless cannot really believe this!' It is possible to imagine the same split attitude towards an Event: 'I know very well there was no Event, just the ordinary run of things, but, perhaps, unfortunately, nonetheless … (I believe) there *was* one.' And – even more interestingly – is it possible for an Event to be not directly denied but denied retroactively? Imagine a society which fully integrated into its ethical substance the great modern axioms of freedom, equality, democratic rights, the duty of a society to provide for education and basic healthcare of all its members, and which rendered racism or sexism simply unacceptable and ridiculous – there is no need even to argue against, say, racism, since anyone who openly advocates racism is immediately perceived as a weird eccentric who cannot be taken seriously. But then, step by step, although society continues to pay lip service to these axioms, they are *de facto* deprived of their substance.

Here is an example from ongoing European history: in the summer of 2012, Viktor Orbán, the Hungarian right-wing PM, said that in Central Europe a new economic system must be built

> and let us hope that God will help us and we will not have to invent a new type of political system instead of democracy that would need to be introduced for the sake of economic survival ... Cooperation is a question of force, not of intention. Perhaps there are countries where things don't work that way, for example in the Scandinavian countries, but such a half-Asiatic rag-tag people as we are can unite only if there is force.[114]

The irony of these lines was not lost on some old Hungarian dissidents: when the Soviet army moved into Budapest to crush the 1956 anti-Communist uprising, the message repeatedly sent by the beleaguered Hungarian leaders to the West was: 'We are defending Europe here!' (against the Asiatic Communists, of course). Now, after Communism has collapsed, the Christian-conservative government paints as its main enemy the multicultural consumerist liberal democracy for which today's Western Europe stands, and calls for a new, more organic communitarian order to replace the 'turbulent' liberal democracy of the last two decades. In the same way that Fascists spoke about 'the plutocratic-Bolshevik plot' (ex-)Communists and liberal 'bourgeois' democrats are perceived as two faces of the same enemy. No wonder Orbán and some of his allies repeatedly express their sympathies for the Chinese 'capitalism with Asian values,' looking to 'Asian' authoritarianism as the solution against the ex-Communist threat – so if Orbán's government finds itself under excessive pressure from the European Union, we can well imagine him sending a message to China: 'We are defending Asia here!'

However, the case of Hungary is just a minor incident in the global process of dis-eventalization which threatens the very fundamentals of our emancipatory achievements. Let's take an example from the other side of our Western world. Here is how, in a letter to the *Los Angeles Times*, director Kathryn Bigelow justified her film *Zero Dark Thirty*'s unflinching look at the torture methods used by U.S. government agents to track down and kill Osama bin Laden: 'Those of us who work in the arts know that depiction is not endorsement. If it was, no artist would be able to paint inhumane practices, no author could write about them, and no filmmaker could delve into the thorny subjects of our time.'[115] Really? Without acting like abstract moralist idealists, and being fully aware of the unpredictable urgencies of fighting terrorist attacks, should we not at least add that torturing a human being is in itself something so profoundly shattering that to depict it neutrally – i.e., to neutralize this shattering dimension – already *is* a kind of endorsement?

More precisely, the catch is: *how* is torture depicted? Since the topic is so sensitive, any kind of actual neutrality in the film's texture is here a fake; a certain stance towards the topic is always discernible. Imagine a documentary on the Holocaust depicting it in a cool disinterested way as a big industrial-logistic operation, dealing with the technical problems (transport, disposal of the bodies, preventing panic among the prisoners to be gassed, etc.) – such a film would either embody a perverse and deeply immoral fascination with its topic, or it would count on the very obscene neutrality of its style to engender dismay and horror in spectators. Where is Bigelow here? Definitely and with no shadow of a doubt on the side of the normalization of torture. When Maya, the film's heroine, first witnesses waterboarding, she is a little bit shocked, but she quickly learns the game – later in the film she coldly blackmails a high-level Arab prisoner: 'If you don't talk to us, we will deliver you to Israel.' Her fanatical pursuit of bin Laden helps to neutralize any ordinary moral qualms. Much more ominous is her partner, a young bearded CIA agent who masters perfectly the art of passing glibly from torture to friendliness after the victim is broken (lighting his cigarette and sharing jokes). There is something deeply disturbing in how, later in the film, he smoothly changes from a bearded torturer in jeans to a well-dressed Washington bureaucrat. *This* is normalization at its purest and most efficient – a little bit of uneasiness, more about hurt sensitivity than about ethics, but the job has to be done. This awareness of the hurt sensitivity as the (main) human cost of torture makes it sure that the film is not just cheap right-wing propaganda: the psychological complexity is properly depicted, so that well-meaning liberals can enjoy the film without feeling guilty. This is why *Zero Dark Thirty* is much worse than *24*, where at least Jack Bauer breaks down at the series' finale.[116]

The debate about waterboarding being torture or not should be dropped as obvious nonsense: why, if not by causing pain and fear of death, does waterboarding make hardened terrorist-suspects talk? As to the replacement of the word 'torture' by 'enhanced interrogation technique,' one should note that we are dealing here with an extension of the logic of Political Correctness: in exactly the same way that 'disabled' becomes 'physically challenged,' 'torture' becomes 'enhanced interrogation technique' (and, presumably, 'rape' could become 'enhanced seduction technique'). The crucial point is that torture – brutal violence practised by the state – was made publicly acceptable at the very moment when public language was rendered Politically Correct in order to protect victims from the symbolic violence of labels. These two phenomena are two sides of the same coin.

The most obscene defence of the film is the claim that Bigelow rejects cheap moralizing and soberly presents the reality of the anti-terrorist struggle, raising difficult questions and thus compelling us to think (plus, some critics add, she 'deconstructs' feminine clichés – Maya displays no sexual interests or sentimentality, she is tough and dedicated to her task like a man). Our answer should be that, precisely apropos a topic like torture, one should not 'think'. A parallel with rape imposes itself here: what if a film were to show a brutal rape in the same neutral way, claiming that one should avoid cheap moralizing and start to think about rape in all its complexity? Our gut instinct tells us that there is something terribly wrong here: I would like to live in a society where rape is simply considered unacceptable, so that anyone who argues for it appears an eccentric idiot, not in a society where one has to argue against it – and the same goes for torture: a sign of ethical progress is the fact that torture is 'dogmatically' rejected as repulsive, without any need for further discussion.

So what about the 'realist' argument: torture was always going on, if anything even more in the (near) past, so is it not better to at least be talking publicly about it? This, exactly, is the problem: if torture was always going on, *why are those in power now telling us about it openly?* There is only one answer: to normalize it, i.e., to lower our ethical standards. Torture saves lives? Maybe, but it loses souls for sure – and its most obscene justification is to claim that a true hero is ready to forsake his/her soul to save the lives of his/her countrymen. The normalization of torture in *Zero Dark Thirty* is a sign of the moral vacuum we are gradually approaching. If there is any doubt about this, just try to imagine a major Hollywood film depicting torture in a similar way twenty or thirty years ago – it's unthinkable.

Let us now jump to our third and much more brutal case, which confronts us with what is unthinkable even today. The documentary *The Act of Killing* (Final Cut Film Productions, Copenhagen) premiered in 2012 at the Telluride film festival. Directed by Joshua Oppenheimer and Christine Cynn, *The Act of Killing* provides a unique and deeply disturbing insight into the ethical deadlock of global capitalism. The documentary – shot in Medan, Indonesia in 2007 – reports on a case of obscenity which reaches the extreme: a film, made by Anwar Congo and his friends, some of whom are now respected politicians but who were gangsters and death squad leaders who played a key role in the killing of around 2.5 million alleged Communist sympathizers, mostly ethnic Chinese, in 1965–66. *The Act of Killing* is about 'killers who have won, and the sort of society they have built'. After their victory, their terrible acts were not relegated to the status of the 'dirty secret,' the founding crime whose traces are to be obliterated – on the contrary, they boast openly about the details of their massacres (the way to strangle a victim with a wire, the way to cut a throat, how to rape a woman in a most pleasurable way). In October 2007, Indonesian state TV produced a talk show celebrating Anwar and his friends; in the middle of the show, after Anwar says that their killings were inspired by gangster movies, the beaming moderator turns to the cameras and says: 'Amazing! Let's give Anwar Congo a round of applause!' When she asks Anwar if he fears the revenge of the victim's relatives, he answers: 'They can't. When they raise their heads, we wipe them out!' His henchman adds: 'We'll exterminate them all!' and the audience explodes into exuberant cheers. One has to see this to believe it.

But what makes *The Act of Killing* extraordinary is that it takes a step further here and asks the key question: what did the killers '*[have] in mind when they were killing people*,'[117] i.e., which protective screen did they use to make them blind to the horror of what they were doing? The answer is that this protective screen which prevented a deeper moral crisis was the cinematic screen: they experienced their activity as an enactment of their cinematic models, which enabled them to experience reality itself as a fiction – as great admirers of Hollywood (they started their career as organizers and controllers of the black market in peddling cinema tickets), they played a role in their massacres, imitating a Hollywood gangster, cowboy or even a musical dancer.

There is a nice joke about Jesus Christ: in order to relax after the arduous work of preaching and performing miracles, Jesus decided to take a short break on the shore of the Galilee Sea. During a game of golf with one of his apostles, he had a difficult shot; Jesus did it badly and the ball ended up in the water, so he did his usual trick, walked on the water to the place where the ball was, reached down and picked it up. When Jesus was about to try the same shot again, the apostle told him that it was a very difficult one – only someone like Tiger Woods could do it. Jesus replied, 'What the hell, I am the son of God, I can do what Tiger Woods can do!' and took another swing. The ball ended up in the water again, so Jesus again took a walk on the surface of the water to retrieve it. At this point, a group of American tourists walked by and one of them, observing what was going on, turned to the apostle and said: 'My god, who is that guy there? Does he think he's Jesus or what?' The apostle replied: 'No, the jerk thinks he's Tiger Woods!' This is how fantasmatic identification works: no one, not even God himself, is directly what he is; everybody needs an external, decentred point of identification. And we can imagine the scene with an American journalist observing Anwar engaged in torturing a suspected Communist: the journalist asks Anwar's friend who's standing by, 'Who is that guy there? Does he think he is an instrument of God's justice?', and the friend replies: 'No, he thinks he's Humphrey Bogart!'

Here we encounter society's moral vacuum at its most brutal: what kind of symbolic texture (the set of rules which draw the line between what is publicly acceptable and what is not) a society must be composed of if even a minimal level of public shame (which would compel the perpetrators to treat their acts as a 'dirty secret') is suspended, and a monstrous orgy of torture and killing can be publicly celebrated even decades after it took place, not even as a extraordinary, necessary crime for the public good, but as an ordinary, acceptable and pleasurable activity? The trap to be avoided here is, of course, the easy one of putting the blame either directly on Hollywood or on the 'ethical primitiveness' of Indonesia. The starting point should rather be the dislocating effects of capitalist globalization which, by undermining the 'symbolic efficacy' of traditional ethical structures, creates such a moral vacuum.[118]

Does this mean that, through the gradual dissolution of our ethical substance, we are simply regressing to individualistic egotism? Things are much more complex. We often hear that our ecological crisis is the result of our short-term egotism: obsessed with immediate pleasures and wealth, we forgot about the common Good. However, it is here that Walter Benjamin's notion of capitalism as religion becomes crucial: a true capitalist is not a hedonistic egotist; he is, on the contrary, fanatically devoted to his task of multiplying his wealth, ready to neglect his health and happiness, not to mention the prosperity of his family and the well-being of the environment. There is thus no need to evoke some high-minded morality and trash capitalist egotism – against capitalist perverted fanatical dedication, it is enough to evoke a good measure of simple egotistic and utilitarian concerns. In other words, the pursuit of what Rousseau calls the natural *amour-de-soi* (love of self) requires a highly civilized level of awareness.

The hedonistic egotism which allegedly pervades our societies is thus not a fact but our societies' ideology – the ideology philosophically articulated in Hegel's *Phenomenology of Spirit* towards the end of the chapter on Reason, under the name of '*das geistige Tierreich*' – the 'spiritual kingdom of animals,' Hegel's name for the modern civil society in which humans are caught in self-interested interaction. As Hegel put it, the achievement of modernity was to allow 'the principle of subjectivity to attain fulfilment in the *self-sufficient extreme* of personal particularity'.[119] This principle makes possible civil society as the domain in which autonomous human individuals associate with each other through the institutions of the free-market economy in order to satisfy their private needs: all communal ends are subordinated to the private interests of individuals; they are consciously posited and calculated with the goal of maximizing the satisfaction of these interests. What matters for Hegel here is the opposition of private and common perceived by those on whom Hegel relies (Mandeville, Adam Smith) as well as by Marx: individuals perceive the common domain as something that should serve their private interests (like a liberal who thinks of the state as a protector of private freedom and safety), while individuals, in pursuing their narrow goals, effectively serve the communal interest. The properly dialectical tension emerges here when we become aware that, the more individuals act egotistically, the more they contribute to the common wealth.

The paradox is that when individuals want to sacrifice their narrow private interests and directly work for the common good, what suffers is the common good itself – Hegel loves to tell historical anecdotes about a good king or prince whose very dedication to the common good brings his country to ruins. The properly philosophical novelty of Hegel was to further determine this 'contradiction' along the lines of the tension between the 'animal' and the 'spiritual': the universal spiritual substance, the 'work of all and everyone,' emerges as the result of the 'mechanical' interaction of individuals. What this means is that the very 'animality' of the self-interested 'human animal' (the individual participating in the complex network of civil society) is the result of the long historical process of the transformation of medieval hierarchic society into modern bourgeois society. It is thus the very fulfilment of the principle of subjectivity – the radical opposite of animality – which brings about the reversal of subjectivity into animality.

Traces of this shift can be detected everywhere today, especially in the fast-developing Asian countries where capitalism exerts a most brutal impact. Bertolt Brecht's 'The Exception and the Rule' (a 'learning play' written in 1929–30 for performance in factories and schools) tells the story of a rich merchant who, with his porter ('coolie'), crosses the Yahi Desert (one of Brecht's fictional Chinese places) to close an oil deal. When the two get lost in the desert and their water supplies are running low, the merchant mistakenly shoots the coolie, thinking he was being attacked, when the coolie was actually offering him some water that he still had left in his bottle. Later, in court, the merchant is acquitted: the judge concludes that the merchant had every right to fear a potential threat from the coolie, so he was justified in shooting him in self-defence regardless of whether there was an actual threat. Since the merchant and his coolie belong to different classes, the merchant had every reason to expect hatred and aggression from him: this is the typical situation, the rule, while the coolie's kindness was an exception. Is this story yet another of Brecht's ridiculous Marxist simplifications? No, judging from this report from today's real China:

In Nanjing, half a decade ago, an elderly woman fell while getting on a bus. Newspaper reports tell us that the 65-year-old woman broke her hip. At the scene, a young man came to her aid; let us call him Peng Yu, for that is his name. Peng Yu gave the elderly woman 200RMB (at that time enough to buy 300 bus tickets) and took her to the hospital. Then, he continued to stay with her until the family arrived. The family sued the young man for 136,419RMB. Indeed, the Nanjing Gulou District Court found the young man to be guilty and ordered him to pay 45,876RMB. The court reasoned, 'according to common sense,' that because Peng Yu was the first off the bus, in all probability he had knocked over the elderly woman. Further, he actually had admitted his guilt, the court reasoned, by staying with the elderly woman at the hospital. It being the case that a normal person would not be as kind as Peng Yu claimed he was.[120]

Is this incident not exactly parallel to Brecht's story? Peng Yu helped the old lady out of simple compassion or decency, but since such a display of goodness is not 'typical,' not the rule ('a normal person would not be as kind as Peng Yu claimed he was'), it was interpreted by the court as proof of Peng Yu's guilt, and he was appropriately punished. Is this a ridiculous exception? Not so, according to the *People's Daily* (the government newspaper), which, in an online opinion poll, asked a large sample of young people what they would do if they were to see an elderly person who had fallen: '87% of young people would not help. Peng Yu's story echoes the surveillance of the public space. People will only help when a camera was present.' What such a reluctance to help signals is a change in the status of public space: 'the street is an intensely private place and seemingly the words public and private make no sense'. In short, being in a public space does not entail only being together with other unknown people – in moving among them, I am still within my private space, engaged in no interaction with or recognition of them. In order to count as public, the space of my co-existence and interaction with others (or the lack of it) has to be covered by security cameras.

Another sign of this same change can be found at the opposite end of watching people die in public and doing nothing – with the recent trend of public sex in hard-core porn. There are more and more films which show a couple (or more persons) engaged in erotic games up to full copulation in heavily frequented public spaces (on a public beach, in a train, at a bus or train station, in the open space of a shopping mall, etc.), and the interesting feature is that a large majority of people who pass by (pretend to) ignore the scene – a minority throw a discreet glance at the couple, even fewer of them make a sarcastic obscene remark. Again, it is as if the copulating couple remain in their private space, so that we should not be concerned by their intimacies.

This brings us back to Hegel's 'spiritual animal kingdom' – that is to say, who effectively behaves like this, passing by dying fellows in blessed ignorance or copulating in front of others? Animals, of course. This fact in no way entails that ridiculous conclusion that we are somehow 'regressing' to the animal level: the animality with which we are dealing here – the ruthless egotism of each of the individuals pursuing his or her private interest – is the paradoxical result of the most complex network of social relations (market exchange, social mediation of production), and the fact that individuals themselves are blind to this complex network points towards its ideal ('spiritual') character: in a civil society structured by the market, abstraction rules more than ever in the history of humanity. It is often said that today, with our total exposure to the media, culture of public confessions and instruments of digital control, private space is disappearing. One should counter this commonplace with the opposite claim: it is the *public* space proper which is disappearing. The person who displays on the web his or her naked images or intimate data and obscene dreams is not an exhibitionist: exhibitionists intrude into the public space, while those who post their naked images on the web remain in their private space and are just expanding it to include others. And, back to *The Act of Killing*, the same goes for Anwar and his colleagues: they are privatizing the public space in a sense which is much more threatening than economic privatization. Such privatization is an exemplary case of how, in our societies, the emancipatory Event of modernity is gradually undone.

FINAL DESTINATION

'Nota Bene!'

What are the chances of an authentic political Event in these depressive conditions in which the predominant process is the undoing of past events? We should begin by reminding ourselves that an Event is a radical turning point, which is, in its true dimension, invisible – to quote French philosopher Maurice Blanchot: 'Q: Will you admit this fact, that we are at a turning point? A: If it's a fact it's not a turning point.'[121] In an Event, things not only change, what changes is the very parameter by which we measure the facts of change, i.e., a turning point changes the entire field within which facts appear. This is crucial to bear in mind today when things change all the time, at an unheard-of frantic speed. However, beneath all this constant change, it is not difficult to discern a rather dull sameness, as if things change so that everything can remain the same – or, as the old French proverb has it: *plus ça change, plus c'est la même chose*. In capitalism, where things have to change all the time to remain the same, the true Event would have been to transform the very principle of change. Such a notion of Event which cannot be reduced to simple change was recently developed by Alain Badiou: a contingency (contingent encounter or occurrence) which converts into necessity,[122] i.e., it gives rise to a universal principle demanding fidelity and hard work for the new Order. An erotic encounter is the Event of love when it changes the lovers' entire lives, organizing them around the construction of the shared life of a couple; in politics, a contingent upheaval (revolt) is an Event when it gives rise to a commitment of the collective subject to a new universal emancipatory project, and thereby sets in motion the patient work of restructuring society.

Can we still imagine such an Event today when, with the new millennium, the Left entered a period of profound crisis? In the years of prospering capitalism, it was easy for the Left to play Cassandra, warning that the prosperity was based on illusions and prophesizing catastrophes to come. Now the economic downturn and social disintegration the Left was waiting for is here, and protests and revolts are popping up all around the globe. But what is conspicuously absent is any consistent Leftist reply to these events, any project of how to transpose islands of chaotic resistance into a positive programme of social change. The rage exploding all around Europe today

> is impotent and inconsequential, as consciousness and coordinated action seem beyond the reach of present society. Look at the European crisis. Never in our life have we faced a situation so charged with revolutionary opportunities. Never in our life have we been so impotent. Never have intellectuals and militants been

so silent, so unable to find a way to show a new possible direction.[123]

In the last couple of years, we thus have dwelt in a continuous pre-evental situation in which an invisible barrier seems to prevent again and again the genesis of a proper Event, the rise of something New. One of the reasons for this invisible barrier is the latest ideological triumph of capitalism: each worker becomes his or her own capitalist, the 'entrepreneur-of-the-self' who decides how much to invest in his or her own future education, health, and so on, paying for these investments by getting indebted. The rights to education, healthcare, housing, etc. thus become free decisions to invest in, which are formally at the same level as the banker's or capitalist's decision to invest in this or that company, so that, at this formal level, everyone is a capitalist getting indebted in order to invest.[124] We are here a step further from the formal equality between the capitalist and the worker in the eyes of the law – now they are both capitalist investors; however, the same difference in the 'physiognomy of our *dramatis personae*' which, according to Marx, appears after the exchange between labour and capital is concluded, reappears here between the capitalist investor proper and the worker who is compelled to act as the 'entrepreneur-of-the-self': 'The one smirks self-importantly and is intent on business; the other is timid and holds back, like someone who has brought his own hide to market and has nothing else to expect but – a tanning.'[125] And he is right to remain timid – the freedom of choice imposed on him is a false one, it is the very form of his servitude.

• • •

How does today's rise of the indebted man, specific to conditions of global capitalism, relate to the relationship of debtor/creditor as a universal anthropological constant articulated by Nietzsche? It is the paradox of direct realization which turns into its opposite. Today's global capitalism brings the relationship of debtor/creditor to its extreme and simultaneously undermines it: debt becomes an openly ridiculous excess. We thus enter the domain of obscenity: when a credit is accorded, the debtor is not even expected to return it – debt is directly treated as a means of control and domination. Take the ongoing EU pressure on Greece to implement austerity measures – this pressure fits perfectly what psychoanalysis calls 'superego'. Superego is not an ethical agency proper, but a sadistic agent that bombards the subject with impossible demands, obscenely enjoying the subject's failure to comply with them; the paradox of the superego is that, as Freud saw it clearly, the more we obey its demands, the more we feel guilty.[126] Imagine a vicious teacher who gives to his pupils impossible tasks, and then sadistically jeers when he sees their anxiety and panic. This is what is so terribly wrong with the EU demands/commands: they don't even give a chance to Greece; Greek failure is part of the game. The goal of politico-economic analysis here is to deploy strategies to step out of this infernal circle of debt and guilt.

A similar paradox was operative from the very beginning, of course, since a promise/obligation which cannot ever be fully met is at the very base of the banking system. When one puts money into a bank, the bank obliges itself to return the money at any point – but we all know that, while the bank can do this for some of the people who deposit money into it, it cannot do so for all of them. However, this paradox, which originally held for the relationship between individuals who deposit money and their bank, now also holds for the relationship between the bank and (legal or physical) persons who borrow money from it. What this implies is that the true aim of lending money to the debtor is not to get the debt repaid with a profit, but the indefinite continuation of the debt which keeps the debtor in permanent dependency and subordination. A decade or so ago, Argentina decided to repay its debt to the International Monetary Fund (IMF) ahead of time (with financial help from Venezuela), and the reaction of the IMF was surprising: instead of being glad that it had got its money back, the IMF (or, rather, its top representatives) expressed their worry that Argentina will use this new freedom and financial independence from international financial institutions to abandon tight fiscal policies and engage in careless spending. This uneasiness made palpable the true stakes of the debtor/creditor relationship: debt is an instrument to control and regulate the debtor, and, as such, it strives for its own expanded reproduction.

So, back to our starting point: how can an Event break us out of this debilitating situation? Perhaps we should begin by effectively renouncing the myth of a Great Awakening – the moment when, if not the old working class then a new alliance of the dispossessed, multitude or whatever, will gather its forces and master a decisive intervention. We should return to Hegel here: a dialectical process begins with some affirmative idea towards which it strives. However, in the course of this striving, *the idea itself undergoes a profound transformation* (not just a tactical accommodation, but an essential redefinition), because the idea itself is caught into the process, (over) determined by its actualization. Say we have a revolt motivated by a request for justice: once people get really engaged in it, they become aware that much more is needed to bring true justice than just the limited requests with which they started (to repeal some laws, etc.). What happens in such moments is a reframing of the universal dimension itself, the imposing of a new universality.

This new universality is not an all-encompassing container, a compromise between disparate forces; it is a universality based on division. President Obama is often accused of dividing the American people instead of bringing them together to find broad bipartisan solutions. But what if this, precisely, is what is good about him? In situations of deep crisis, an authentic division is urgently needed – a division between those who want to drag on within the old parameters and those who are aware of the necessary change. Such a division, not opportunistic compromises, is the only path to true unity.

Furthermore, we should not be afraid to reassert two other notions which are implied by division: hatred and violence. 'Politics is organized hatred that is unity.' This sentence comes from John Jay Chapman (1862–1933), today a half-forgotten American political activist and essayist who also early discerned the lie of charity: 'The general cowardice of this age covers itself with the illusion of charity, and asks, in the name of Christ, that no one's feelings be hurt.'[127] The notion of politics as organized hatred is far from totalitarian madness – here is its contemporary version:

> The situation thus clarifies itself at this point: we have enemies. They are not necessarily hostile towards us, it can even be that they sincerely wish for us to be happy, thriving and proud to live in the world they conceived for us. One can even say that it is exactly this that they expect from us: to confirm to them that their world is the best of all possible worlds – or the least bad, it depends on the case.[128]

Once, decades ago, liberals were saying this about Communists – today, it holds for the enemies of Communism. Does this mean we advocate a blind violence? One should demystify the problem of violence, rejecting simplistic claims that twentieth-century Communism used too much excessive murderous violence, and that we should be careful not to fall into this trap again. As a fact, this is, of course, terrifyingly true, but such a direct focus on violence obfuscates the underlying question: what was wrong in the twentieth-century Communist project as such? Which inherent weakness of this project pushed the Communists in power (and not only those) to resort to unrestrained violence? In other words, it is not enough to say that Communists 'neglected the problem of violence': it was a deeper socio-political failure which pushed them to violence. (The same goes for the notion that Communists 'neglected democracy': their overall project of social transformation enforced on them this 'neglect'.) The Chinese Cultural Revolution serves as a lesson here: destroying old monuments proved not to be a true negation of the past. Rather it was an impotent *passage à l'acte*, an 'acting out' which bore witness to the failure to get rid of the past.

When the Romanian writer Panait Istrati visited the Soviet Union in the late 1920s, when the first big purges and show trials began, a Soviet apologist, trying to convince him about the need for violence against their enemies, evoked the proverb 'You can't make an omelette without breaking any eggs,' to which Istrati tersely replied: 'All right. I can see the broken eggs. Where's this omelette of yours?'[129] He was right, but not just in the usual sense of rejecting raw violence which cannot be justified by its results. The true 'breaking the eggs' is not physical violence, but the intervention into social and ideological relations which, without necessarily destroying anything or anyone, transforms the entire symbolic field – how? To conclude, let us take our last example from cinema, the Greek film *Strella* by Panos Koutras (2009).

After being rejected by state funding bodies and turned down by all the major production companies, Koutras was obliged to make his film without any financial support whatsoever, and so *Strella* became a completely independent production with nearly all the roles played by non-professionals. However, the result was a cult movie winning numerous prizes. Here is the story: Yiorgos is released from prison after fourteen years of incarceration for a murder he committed in his small village. (He found his seventeen-year-old brother playing sex games with his five-year-old son and, in a fit of rage, he killed him.) During his long stay in prison, he lost contact with his son, Leonidas, whom he now tries to trace. He spends his first night of freedom in a cheap downtown hotel in Athens, where he meets Strella, a young transsexual prostitute. They spend the night together and soon they fall in love. Yiorgos is accepted by Strella's circle of tranny friends, and he admires her impersonation of Maria Callas. However, he soon discovers that Strella is in fact his son Leonidas: what's more, she knew Yiorgos was her father the whole time, was following him when he left prison, and waited for him in the corridor of the hotel. At first she just wanted to see him, but after he made a pass at her, she went along with it. Traumatized, Yiorgos runs away and breaks down, but the couple re-establish contact and discover that, in spite of the impossibility of continuing their sexual relationship, they really care for each other. Gradually, they find a *modus vivendi*, and the final scene takes place at a New Year celebration: Strella, her friends and Yiorgos all gather at her place, with a small child that Strella decides to take care of, the son of a dead friend of hers. The child gives body to their love *and* to the deadlock of their relationship.

Strella brings perversion to its (ridiculously sublime) end: the traumatic discovery is repeated. First, early in the film, Yiorgos discovers that the beloved/desired woman is a transvestite and accepts this without further ado, with no pathetic shock: when he notices that his partner is a man, the partner simply says, 'I am a tranny. Do you have a problem with that?', and they go on kissing and embracing. What follows is the truly traumatic discovery that Strella is his own son he was looking for and who knowingly seduced him. Here, Yiorgos's reaction is the same as Fergus's when he sees Dil's penis in *The Crying Game*: shattering disgust, escape, wandering around in the city unable to cope with what he discovered. The outcome is also similar to *The Crying Game*: the trauma is overcome through love; a happy family with a small son emerges.

Production notes describe *Strella* as 'the kind of story told at dinner parties, a kind of urban legend' – which means that we should not read it in the same way as *The Crying Game*: the hero's discovery that his transsexual lover is his son is not the actualization of some unconscious fantasy, his reaction of disgust is truly just the reaction to an external bad surprise. In other words, we should resist the temptation to mobilize the psychoanalytic apparatus and interpret the father-son incest: there is nothing to interpret, the situation at the film's end is *completely normal*, the situation of genuine family happiness. As such, the film serves as a test for the advocates of Christian family values: embrace *this* authentic family of Yiorgos, Strella and the adopted child, or shut up about Christianity. The family that emerges at the film's end is a proper sacred family, something like God the Father living with Christ and fucking him, the ultimate gay marriage *and* parental incest – a triumphant reframing of the fantasy.[130] In his *Notes Towards a Definition of Culture*, T. S. Eliot remarked that there are moments when the only choice is the one between heresy and non-belief, when the only way to keep a religion alive is to perform a sectarian split from its main corps. Exactly the same holds for the Christian family values: the only way to redeem them is to redefine or reframe family so that it includes the situation at the end of *Strella* as its exemplary case.

This, then, is the end – it has brought us back to the beginning, to our first definition of Event as the act of reframing, from which we continued our journey through Event as Fall, Event as Enlightenment, the three philosophical Events and the three aspects of Event in psychoanalysis. After confronting the possibility of undoing an Event, we reached our final destination by outlining the contours of a political Event.[131] If, late in the evening, already in bed, the traveller who has just finished this journey is pleasantly tired or too exhausted to envisage the prospect of a political Event, I can only say to him sincerely: '*Nota bene!*'

Notes

1. This is why when in love we expose ourselves to the beloved in all our vulnerability: when we are naked together, a cynical smile or remark from our partner may turn charm into ridicule. Love implies absolute trust: in loving another, I give him or her the power to destroy me, hoping/trusting s/he will not use this power.
2. See Marc Vernet, 'Film Noir on the Edge of Doom,' in Joan Copjec, ed., *Shades of Noir*, London: Verso Books, 1993.
3. Stephen Hawking and Leonard Mlodinow, *The Grand Design*, New York: Bantam, 2010, p. 5.
4. In spite of the ridicule of the whole enterprise, there is a kind of tragic beauty in it; in his *D'un château à l'autre*, Céline provides a vivid description of the misery and confusion of daily life at Sigmaringen.
5. For a simple introduction to Lacan's work, see Slavoj Žižek, *How to Read Lacan*, London: Granta Books, 2006.
6. Quoted from www.friesian.com/hist-2.htm.
7. A more specific version of the same formula can be found in the so-called 'parallel opera films,' in which a contemporary story parallels the plot of an opera (usually a popular Italian one) the staging of which is the focal point of the film's plot. *Il Sogno di Butterfly* (*Butterfly's Dream*), an Italian film from 1939, provides an interesting version of this procedure: Rosa, who sings on stage Cio-Cio San, falls in love with an American tenor who goes back to the United States without knowing that she is pregnant. Four years later, now rich and famous and with an American wife, he returns to Italy; but unlike her operatic counterpart, Rosa does not kill herself – she rather dedicates her life to her young son.
8. The persistence of this formula of the production of a couple is

quite surprising – in *Argo* (2012), we learn at the beginning that the CIA agent who organizes the escape from Iran of six U.S. embassy employees hidden in the house of the Canadian ambassador lives separated from his wife, although he is very attached to his small son. At the film's end, in the very last scene, he approaches the house where his wife lives and asks her if he can enter; she silently embraces him. The mystery of this scene is that, since it directly follows his professional triumph, it appears that his estranged wife somehow learned about his heroic patriotic act and is ready to take him back in gratitude – but she cannot know anything about it, since the participation of the CIA in the operation was secret. The underlying logic of the film is thus, yet again, that its actual core is not how to save the hiding U.S. employees but the unification of the couple.

9. In Lorene Scafaria's *Seeking a Friend for the End of the World* (2012), we also learn that an asteroid nearing the Earth will kill all life on it in three weeks; however, although the catastrophe is real and inevitable, it still serves as a vehicle to create a couple who, minutes before the catastrophe, acknowledge their love and then vanish embraced. The film's message is thus: it takes a total catastrophe to create a real couple.

10. Another detail: when the Thing approaches Earth, not only does the behaviour of animals become odd (horses get disturbed, etc.), but also the atmosphere changes: for a short time, Justine and Claire sweat and find it difficult to breathe – the basic co-ordinates of nature, of its balance, are disintegrating.

11. In Benigni's film, Guido, a Jewish father, and his small son Joshua are arrested by the Germans and put into Auschwitz. To make life in the camp bearable for Joshua, Guido convinces him that the camp is a complicated game in which Joshua must perform the tasks Guido gives him, earning him points; the first team to reach 1,000 points will win a tank. He tells him that if he cries, complains that he wants his mother, or says that he is hungry, he will lose points, while quiet boys who hide from the camp guards earn extra points. To see what is wrong with the film one has to make a simple mental experiment: to imagine the same film with one change – at the end, Guido would have learned that Joshua knew all the time where he was, in a concentration camp, and that he just pretended that he believed in Guido's story to make life easier for him.

12. And let us not forget that, in a sense which is far from crazy but concerns our innermost elementary experience, Justine is *right*: life *is* a disgusting thing, a sleazy object moving out of itself, secreting humid warmth, crawling, stinking, growing. The birth itself of a human being is an *Alien*-like event: a monstrous event of something erupting out from the inside of a body, a moving, big hairy body. It should all disappear. Spirit is above life, it is death in life, an attempt to escape life while alive, like the Freudian death-drive which is not life but a pure repetitive movement.
13. A noteworthy detail in *The Tree of Life* is the formula it provides for resolving the Oedipal tension: father and son are reconciled when, after the father apologizes for being a bad father, his son replies: 'I'm as evil as you are.' *This* is the correct formula of paternal identification: I no longer try to identify with the father as ideal, I identify with his very failure to be a good father.
14. Quoted from www.huffingtonpost.com/rabbi-david-wolpe/tree-of-life_b_868717.html.
15. Peter Wessel Zapffe, *Om det tragiske*, Oslo: De norske bokklubbene, 2004, p. 147.
16. Giorgio Agamben, *Stanzas*, Minneapolis: University of Minnesota Press, 1993, p. 20.
17. Pauline Kael, *5001 Nights at the Movies*, New York: Macmillan, 1991, p. 107.
18. Similar, but not the same, is the case of Raphael Siboni's documentary with a Lacanian title, *Il n'y a pas de rapport sexuel* (2012). The film is much more than a 'making of' a hardcore porn movie: by way of following from a minimal distance the shooting of a hardcore film, i.e., by way of stepping back and rendering visible the frame, the window through which we observe the scene, it totally desexualizes the entire scene, presenting hardcore acting as grey repetitive work: faking ecstatic pleasure, masturbating offscene to retain an erection, smoking during the breaks, etc.
19. Richard Boothby, *Freud as Philosopher*, New York: Routledge, 2001, pp. 275–76.
20. Søren Kierkegaard, *Fear and Trembling / Repetition*, Princeton: Princeton University Press, 1983, p. 162. I am indebted to Mladen Dolar for this reference to Kierkegaard, Heine and Marx.

21. Stalin's position seems ambiguous here: one can imagine a Stalinist purge as the effort to liquidate all chimney sweepers who disturb the socialist harmony – but was Stalin himself also not the supreme sweeper?
22. One should also not forget that a maid and a chimney sweeper themselves form a couple – recall the old myth of chimney sweepers as the seducers of innocent maids.
23. See Walter Benjamin, 'On Language as Such and on the Language of Man' (1916), in *One-Way Street and Other Writings*, London: New Left Books, 1979, pp. 107–23.
24. In the 2012 blockbuster *The Wrath of the Titans* there is an interesting line when one of the gods claims that humans are immortal, because after their death they continue to live (in their immortal soul or in tradition), while only gods are truly mortal: when they die, they really disappear, nothing remains. Heidegger's couple of mortals and immortals should thus be turned around: human immortals versus mortal gods.
25. Christianity thus enjoins us to reverse the terms of the 'king's two bodies': God himself has two bodies, but in crucifixion, it is not the terrestrial body which dies, while the sublime body remains as the Holy Spirit; what dies on the cross is the very sublime body of Christ.
26. G. K. Chesterton, *Orthodoxy*, San Francisco: Ignatius Press, 1995, p. 139.
27. *De cultu feminarum*, section I.I, part 2; quoted from www.tertullian.org/anf/anf04/anf04-06.htm#P265_52058.
28. G. K. Chesterton, *Saint Francis of Assisi*, New York: Empire Books, 2012, pp. 11–12.
29. Schelling made the same point when he emphasized how, in the Ancient Roman Empire, the rise of Christianity was preceded by the rise of decadence and corruption.
30. G.W.F. Hegel, *Vorlesungen über die Philosophie der Religion II*, Frankfurt: Suhrkamp Verlag, 1969, p. 205.
31. *Hegel's Science of Logic*, Atlantic Highlands: Humanities Press, 1969, p. 402.
32. Ray Kurzweil, *The Singularity Is Near*, New York: Penguin Books, 2006, p. 9.

33. Brian Greene, *The Elegant Universe*, New York: Norton, 1999, pp. 116–19.
34. Ibid., p. 171.
35. Kojin Karatani, *History and Repetition*, New York: Columbia University Press, 2011, pp. 196–97.
36. Ibid., p. 197.
37. Before we dismiss Ussher's work as a ridiculous curiosity, we should remember that, until a couple of years ago, the Gideon Bible available in most hotels included his chronology of creation!
38. François Balmès, *Structure, logique, aliénation*, Toulouse: Érès, 2011, p. 16.
39. I rely here on Ahmed El Hady's 'Neurotechnology, Social Control and Revolution,' available online at bigthink.com/ideas/neurotechnology-social-control-and-revolution?page=all.
40. Quoted from Ahmed El Hady, op.cit.
41. www.post-gazette.com/pg/11283/1181062-53.stm.
42. The text was written towards the end of 1925, but it was first published decades later. The only available translation is in German: Andrei Platonov, 'Der Antisexus,' in Boris Groys and Aage Hansen-Loeve, eds., *Am Nullpunkt*, Frankfurt: Suhrkamp Verlag, 2005, pp. 494–505. As a curiosum one should add that, in August 2012, a deputy of the Moscow Duma, Vladimir Platonov, became known as 'anti-sexus' for his advocacy of the prohibition of all sexual education and propaganda (as detrimental to public health and morality) in Russian public media and schools – from Andrei to Vladimir, this is arguably the most succinct formula of the decay of public life in Russia.
43. Mladen Dolar, 'Telephone and Psychoanalysis,' *Filozofski vestnik*, No. 1, 2008, p. 12 (in Slovene).
44. C. E. Elger, A. D. Friederici, C. Koch, H. Luhmann, C. von der Malsburg, R. Menzel, H. Monyer, F. Rösler, G. Roth, H. Scheich and W. Singer, 'Das Manifest: Elf führende Neurowissenschaftler über Gegenwart und Zukunft der Hirnforschung,' *Gehirn und Geist*, Vol. 6, 2004, p. 37.
45. Jürgen Habermas, 'The language game of responsible agency and the problem of free will: how can epistemic dualism be reconciled with

ontological monism?', *Philosophical Explorations*, Vol. 10, No. 1, March 2007, p. 31.

46. See Thomas Metzinger, *Being No One: The Self-Model Theory of Subjectivity*, Cambridge, Mass.: MIT Press, 2003.
47. A clear sign of this pragmatic approach is the role of meditation in Buddhism: while in the West, meditation is perceived as central (one of the relaxation techniques to achieve 'inner peace'), so that to be a Buddhist effectively means to practise meditation, in the East, where Buddhism really is a way of life, only a tiny minority engages in meditation – the majority just (pretends to) follow(s) the ethical norms imposed by Buddhism (kindness, no suffering, etc.). Monks who fully meditate serve as a kind of 'subject supposed to meditate,' a guarantee (to ordinary people) that Enlightenment is possible.
48. See Michael Jerryson and Mark Jürgensmeyer, *Buddhist Warfare*, Oxford: Oxford University Press, 2010.
49. Mark Epstein, *Thoughts Without a Thinker*, New York: Basic Books, 1996, p. 83.
50. Ibid., p. 211.
51. Owen Flanagan, *The Boddhisattva's Brain: Buddhism Naturalized*, Cambridge, Mass.: MIT Press, 2011, p. 160.
52. Quoted from Elaine Feinstein, *Ted Hughes*, London: Weidenfeld & Nicolson, 2001, p. 166.
53. Quoted from Feinstein, op.cit., p. 234.
54. Available online at thinkexist.com/quotes/neilgaiman.
55. W. B. Yeats, 'He Wishes for the Cloths of Heaven' (1899).
56. Immanuel Kant, 'The Conflict of Faculties,' in *Political Writings*, Cambridge: Cambridge University Press, 1991, p. 182.
57. Jorge Semprún, *The Long Voyage*, Los Angeles: Overlook TP, 2005, p. 172.
58. Marcus Aurelius, *Meditations*, Book 6, p. 13, quoted from classics.mit.edu/Antoninus/meditations.html.
59. Søren Kierkegaard, *Works of Love*, New York: Harper Torchbooks, 1962, p. 114.
60. One should also note that, from the very beginning, Descartes' thought

echoed among women – '*cogito* has no sex' was the reaction of an early female reader. The person who first deployed this feminist potential of Cartesianism was François Poullain de la Barre, a follower of Descartes who, after becoming a priest, converted to Protestantism. He applied Cartesian principles to the question of the sexes and denounced injustice against women and the inequality of the female condition, championing social equality between women and men. In 1673, he published anonymously *De l'Égalité des Deux Sexes: Discours physique et moral où l'on voit l'importance de se défaire des préjugés* (A Physical and Moral Discourse on the Equality of both Sexes, which shows that it is important to rid oneself of Prejudices), showing that the inequality between the sexes does not have a natural base but proceeds from cultural prejudice. He also recommended that women receive a proper education and that all careers should be open to them, including scientific ones.

61. G.W.F. Hegel, 'Jenaer Realphilosophie,' in *Fruehe politische Systeme*, Frankfurt: Ullstein, 1974, p. 204; quote from Donald Phillip Verene, *Hegel's Recollection*, Albany, NY: SUNY Press, 1985, pp. 7–8. In *Encyclopaedia* also, Hegel mentions the 'night-like abyss within which a world of infinitely numerous images and presentations is preserved without being in consciousness' (*Encyclopaedia*, para. 453). Hegel's historical source is here Jacob Bohme.
62. Hegel, 'Jenaer Realphilosophie,' op. cit.
63. See Sigmund Freud, 'Psychoanalytic notes upon an autobiographical account of a case of paranoia,' in *Three Case Histories*, New York: Touchstone, 1996.
64. See Catherine Malabou, *Les nouveaux blesses*, Paris: Bayard, 2007.
65. Ibid., p. 315.
66. G. K. Chesterton, *The Man Who Was Thursday*, Harmondsworth: Penguin Books, 1986, pp. 44–45.
67. G. K. Chesterton, 'A Defense of Detective Stories,' in H. Haycraft, ed., *The Art of the Mystery Story*, New York: The Universal Library, 1946, p. 6.
68. Richard Wagner, *Jesus of Nazareth and Other Writings*, Lincoln, Nebr., and London: University of Nebraska Press, 1995, p. 303.
69. Ludwig Feuerbach (1804–72) was a German philosopher who rejected

Hegel's idealism and argued for the full assertion of the human bodily and sensual existence; for him, religion is a fantasy into which humanity projects its own best features.

70. Wagner, *Jesus of Nazareth*, op. cit., pp. 303–304.
71. Jean-Pierre Dupuy, 'Quand je mourrai, rien de notre amour n'aura jamais existé,' unpublished lecture at the colloquium *Vertigo et la philosophie*, École Normale Supérieure, Paris, 14 October 2005.
72. For a more detailed elaboration of this line of thought of Bergson, see Chapter 9 of Slavoj Žižek, *In Defense of Lost Causes*, London: Verso Books, 2007.
73. Rosa Luxemburg, *Reform or Revolution*, Chapter VIII, quoted from www.marxists.org/archive/luxemburg/1900/reform-revolution/ch08.htm.
74. This is what, perhaps, makes problematic the practice of short analysis sessions introduced by Lacan. The idea is clear: Lacan noticed that, in the standard 50-minute psychoanalytic session, the patient just goes over and over things, and that it is only in the last few minutes, when the shadow of the end, of being cut off by the analyst, is close that he or she gets into a panic and produces some valuable material. So the idea came to him: why not simply skip the long period of lost time and limit the session to the last few minutes when, under time pressure, something really happens? The problem here is: can we really get only the productive final part without the preceding 45 minutes of lost time which functions as the time of gestation for the content that explodes in the last five minutes?
75. G.W.H. Hegel, *Philosophie des subjektiven Geistes*, Dordrecht: Riedel, 1978, pp. 6–7.
76. Walter Benjamin (1892–1940) was a German philosopher and art theorist who combined Marxism with Jewish Messianic thought.
77. Benjamin, *The Arcades Project*, Cambridge, Mass.: Belknap Press, 1999, p. 482.
78. Benjamin, *Illuminations*, New York: Schocken Books, 2007, p. 254.
79. However, when Shakespeare speaks of 'a sick man's appetite, who desires most that which would increase his evil' (*Coriolanus*), the ambiguity is radical: this characterization holds for self-destructive evil as well as for the dedication to the Good which neglects one's own well-being.

80. The second part of the argument is no less interesting, with its Nietzschean line of argumentation – not so much the last two lines (with their standard wisdom: fear makes you see what is not there, it makes you misperceive a simple bush in the night as a bear), but rather the more precise previous lines: imagination substantializes a property (feature, emotion), imagining its bearer, its cause.
81. See Karl Popper, *Objective Knowledge*, Oxford: Oxford University Press, 1972.
82. François Balmès, *Structure, logique, aliénation*, Toulouse: Érès, 2011, p. 16.
83. Emmanuel Levinas (1906–95) was a French philosopher and Jewish theologist who focused on the ethical topic of our responsibility to the Other.
84. Jürgen Habermas, *The Future of Human Nature*, Cambridge: Polity Press, 2003, p. 110.
85. Jacques Lacan, *Écrits*, New York: Norton, 2007, p. 824.
86. French writer and anthropologist Georges Bataille (1897–1962) dealt with topics of sexuality, violence and sacrifice.
87. Sergei Eisenstein, 'The Milk Separator and the Holy Grail,' in *Non-Indifferent Nature*, Cambridge: Cambridge University Press, 1987.
88. Quoted from Robert Service, *Lenin*, London: Macmillan, 2000, p. 232.
89. Translated by John Ashbery.
90. Karl Marx and Friedrich Engels, *Selected Works*, Vol. 1, Moscow: Progress Publishers, 1969, p. 83.
91. James Williams, *Gilles Deleuze's* Difference and Repetition*: A Critical Introduction and Guide*, Edinburgh: Edinburgh University Press, 2003, p. 94.
92. Gilles Deleuze, *Difference and Repetition*, London: Continuum Books, 2001, p. 81.
93. Williams, *Gilles Deleuze*, op. cit., p. 96.
94. T. S. Eliot, 'Tradition and the Individual Talent,' in *The Sacred Wood: Essays on Poetry and Criticism*, London: Faber & Faber, 1997 (first published 1921).
95. Jorge Luis Borges, *Other Inquisitions: 1937–52*, New York: Washington Square Press, 1966, p. 113.
96. See Peter Hallward, *Out of This World*, London: Verso Books, 2006.

97. Gilles Deleuze and Felix Guattari, *What Is Philosophy?*, New York: Columbia University Press, 1994, p. 159.
98. Hallward, *Out of This World*, op. cit., p. 54.
99. Williams, *Gilles Deleuze*, op. cit., p. 109.
100. Ibid., p. 87.
101. Jacques Lacan, *Encore*, New York: Norton, 1998, p. 144.
102. Jean-Pierre Dupuy, *Petite métaphysique des tsunamis*, Paris: Seuil, 2005, p. 19.
103. www.marxists.org/reference/archive/hegel/works/ph/phc2b2a.htm.
104. See Ryszard Kapuściński, *Shah of Shahs*, New York: Vintage Books, 1992.
105. See Benjamin Libet, *Mind Time*, Cambridge, Mass.: Harvard University Press, 2005.
106. For this idea, see David J. Levin, *Richard Wagner, Fritz Lang, and the Nibelungen*, Princeton: Princeton University Press, 1998.
107. In his seminar on Wagner at the École Normale Supérieure in Paris, 14 May 2005.
108. Gilles Deleuze, *The Logic of Sense*, New York: Columbia University Press, 1990, p. 5.
109. Ibid., p. 7.
110. See Robert Pirsig, *Zen and the Art of Motorcycle Maintenance*, New York: Bantam, 1984 (first published 1977).
111. Quoted from Brian Victoria, *Zen at War*, New York: Weatherhill, 1998, p. 110.
112. Personal information from a friend.
113. Quoted from Niall Ferguson, *The War of the World*, London: Penguin Books, 2007, p. 623.
114. Quoted from www.presseurop.eu/en/content/news-brief/2437991-orban-considers-alternative-democracy.
115. See www.latimes.com/entertainment/movies/moviesnow/la-et-mn-0116-bigelow-zero-dark-thirty-20130116,0,5937785.story.
116. That's why Bigelow's statement apropos the film – 'When you watch violence, you're being deconstructed in a Lacanian sense' (see www.newyorker.com/talk/2012/12/17/121217ta_talk_filkins) – is not only non-sense (there is no Lacanian deconstruction, Lacan was not a deconstructionist) but an ethical obscenity.
117. Quoted from the publicity material of Final Cut Film Productions.

118. More generally, how can (relatively) decent people do horrible things? To account for this, one should turn around the standard conservative anti-individualist view, according to which social institutions control and contain our individual spontaneous evil tendencies to follow ruthlessly our destructive and egotistical strivings: what if, on the contrary, we as individuals are (relatively) decent, and institutions have to apply all their subterfuge to make us do horrible things? The role of institutions as agents of mediation is crucial here: there are things I would never be able to do directly, in person, but if I leave it to my agents to do it for me I can pretend not to know what is going on. How many humanitarians, from Angelina Jolie and Brad Pitt onwards, invest their money in housing projects in Dubai which employ modern versions of slave labour, while they (can pretend that they) don't know about it, that it was done by their financial advisers, etc.?
119. G.W.F. Hegel, *Elements of the Philosophy of Right*, Cambridge: Cambridge University Press, 1991, para. 260.
120. Michael Yuen, 'China and the Mist of Complicated Things,' unpublished text.
121. Maurice Blanchot's self-interview in *La nouvelle revue Française*, April 1960.
122. See Alain Badiou, *Being and Event*, New York: Continuum, 2007, and *Logics of Worlds*, New York: Continuum, 2009.
123. Franco Bifo Berardi, *After the Future*, Oakland: AK Press, 2011, p. 175.
124. See Mauricio Lazzarato, *The Making of the Indebted Man*, Cambridge, Mass.: MIT Press, 2012.
125 Karl Marx, *Capital*, Vol. 1, London: Penguin Books, 1990, p. 280.
126 It is easy to discern the same superego paradox in the hatred of Muslim fundamentalists for Western liberals: liberals are hated not because they are arrogant and racist towards Islam, but for precisely the opposite reason – because they feel guilty towards the Third World and doubt their own right to be what they are. In this way they are caught in the classic superego predicament – the more they feel guilty, the more viciously they are blamed and accused of hypocrisy.
127 John Jay Chapman, *Practical Agitation*, New York: Charles Scribner & Sons, 1900, p. 47.
128 *Communisme: un manifeste*, Paris: Nous, 2012, p. 9.

129 Andrei Platonov's classic Soviet dystopia novel *The Foundation Pit* (1929–30) tells the story of a group of workers engaged in digging out a huge foundation pit, on the base of which a gigantic house for the working class of the town will be built; but the house will never be built, all that remains is the gigantic hole which obliterated old houses previously occupying that place – could the novel's title also not have been *The Broken Eggs Without the Omelette*?

130 A more detailed analysis of *Strella* should also mention the way the film plays with the status of voice. Strella is an admirer of Maria Callas, imitating her in transvestite clubs. In the film's penultimate scene, after reconciling herself with Yiorgos, Strella walks the night streets of Athens, with a pathetic big hit Puccini aria sung by Callas heard offscreen. Strella has no longer to imitate the singing of Callas – at the end, she accepts her alienation: the voice doesn't have to be yours, instead of you yourself imitating the Other, you accept the other in its otherness.

131 This overview was, of course, far from complete. Among notions of event that we left out, we should mention at least two: the status of Event in analytic philosophy from early Ludwig Wittgenstein to Donald Davidson, and the evental status of quantum processes (waves, etc.) in contemporary subatomic physics.